WALKING
OLD RAILWAYS

Christopher Somerville

DAVID & CHARLES
NEWTON ABBOT   LONDON   NORTH POMFRET (VT)

To J.A.F.S.

The Author wishes to emphasise that walkers should gain permission from the owner before entering any disused railway land.

British Library Cataloguing in Publication Data

Somerville, Christopher
  Walking old railways.
  1. Railroads—Great Britain—Abandonment
  I. Title
  385'.0941   HE3014

  ISBN 0–7153–7681–0

Library of Congress Catalog Card Number 78–74078

First published 1979
Second impression 1979

© Christopher Somerville 1979

Set and printed in Great Britain
by Biddles Limited, Guildford, Surrey
for David & Charles (Publishers) Limited
Brunel House Newton Abbot Devon

Published in the United States of America
by David & Charles Inc
North Pomfret Vermont 05053 USA

CONTENTS

PART I
The joy of walking

1 MAKING TRACKS

'LONDON & SOUTH WESTERN RAILWAY. BEWARE OF TRAINS'

The cast-iron sign leans out from a clump of brambles, flaking and rusty. A line of weather-eaten concrete posts makes a rough margin to the weed-strewn track, which curves away between banks of ferns and rosebay willowherb. Butterflies skim between the wild flowers. High overhead, a buzzard circles patiently, waiting for the walker to put away the map and trudge on, before winging in on its prey.

Walking old railways—a strenuous hobby, laden with discomforts and full of delights. Look at any Ordnance Survey map and you can pick out the dotted lines labelled 'Cse of old Rly', linking towns and villages through the countryside. Follow them on the ground and the neat oblongs of green reveal themselves as stretches of tangled woodland. The thin blue threads become winding streams, where anglers once cursed the busy engines that clanked across the bridges and disturbed the fish.

Walking through the outskirts of country towns, abandoned stations shape themselves out of rotting brick and wood under a heavy disguise of blackberry bushes. Platforms gently crumble in silence. The station master's roses, once his prize-winning pride and joy, now twine round old drooping signal posts, and push their way through gaps in the tarred iron fence.

Toller Porcorum, Wiveliscombe, Slaggyford and Hinton Green are among the many delightfully named self-contained centres in the heart of rural England, where the railway builders once saw opportunities for expansion, and grasped them. Passengers, livestock, milk and vegetables crossed and re-crossed the country on their own intricate mesh of lines. Today the main railway routes prepare for 125 or 150 mph blue-and-grey Inter-City bullets. In contrast, the cross-country and branch lines of the past virtually died with the end of the steam locomotive. A few have survived as railways either as part of the national network, or preserved as steam tourist attractions. For the rest, rails are but a memory and we are left with a system of tracks where the walker can wander to his heart's content.

I took to these man-made highways through the countryside a few years ago. Five long days brought me seventy miles from Bath to Bournemouth, following the route of the much-loved Somerset & Dorset Railway which fell to the Beeching axe in 1966. I stumbled down lush embankments, crossed lofty viaducts of grey Mendip stone, lazed in water-meadows, strode for miles between cornfields and beech-woods. I saw foxes, herons, curlew, woodpeckers, kingfishers; wildlife has returned to the closed lines, finding good hunting and safe lodging in the deserted banks and undergrowth. I bruised my feet, was boiled and soaked, lost my way and sweated gallons. What a feeling, arriving at last at the site of Bournemouth West station—glorious elation and total exhaustion! Many old railways and hundreds of miles later, I'm hooked more firmly than ever.

Most walks are on little branch lines, always prime candidates for closure; they are usually between five and fifteen miles, and offer a good day's walk. Railway relics abound: notices, buildings, bridges and tunnels are all witnesses to the sturdy, confident heyday of steam and iron. Research in the newspaper cuttings section of the local library will bring to light many details about the line chosen by the walker, and he can often find out more from conversations in pubs along the route. Railway lines make fairly level walking, and embankments provide splendid grandstands from which to view the countryside. When interest flags in local flora and fauna, architecture and surroundings, the clandestine joys of nostalgia spur on tired feet for miles.

Old railway walking is not all jam, of course. Many bridges over roads and rivers have been dismantled; stretches of track can be wired up by occupants who do not welcome ramblers. Miles on foot over ankle-turning ballast can pepper unsuitably shod feet with blisters. But the delights—historical, naturalistic, escapist—far outweigh the disadvantages.

6

My object in the following chapters is to spur others to embark on this fascinating pursuit. By the time you have turned the final page, I hope you will be reaching for your stoutest boots, and seeking out on your map, for the first of many times, a 'Cse of old Rly' to conquer.

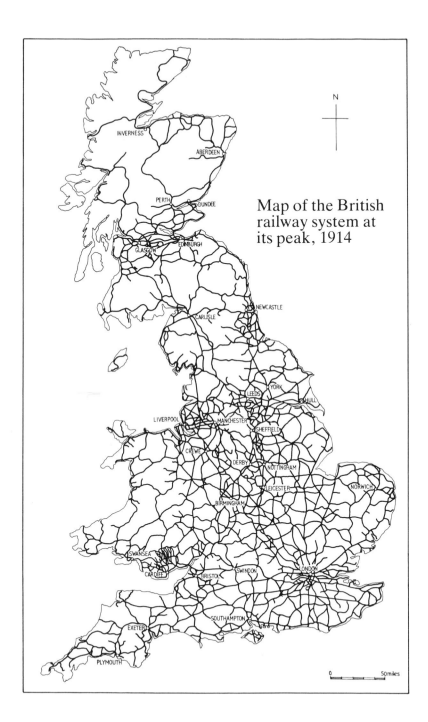

Map of the British railway system at its peak, 1914

2 CLOSURE, OWNERSHIP AND ACCESS

Before discussing in detail the mechanics of walking old railways, it is worth reviewing the events without which there would be no old railways to walk—the closing of uneconomic lines, and subsequent negotiations for purchase of the derelict land.

After the opening of the Stockton & Darlington Railway in 1825, railways expanded rapidly. Isolated towns were linked together and hitherto secluded countryside was opened up. The mobility which the railways brought produced profound social changes in a country still reeling under the impact of the Industrial Revolution. People suddenly claimed travel and communication as their right. Mid-Victorian years saw the construction of much of the British railway network, but growth continued at a slower pace to the end of the nineteenth century and just into the twentieth century.

Two main factors then contributed to a gradual decline of the railways which has not been checked up to the present day; first the development of the motor car, and second the elimination of competition by the grouping of railways in 1923. In the years between the wars private motoring which brought benefits and freedom as regards timing and destination of the journey to the individual as opposed to a *dictat* by the railway companies began its relentless expansion. Moreover buses were found to be much more flexible than trains on certain routes and took the traffic from the railways, although today even buses have lost out to private cars.

The other factor was the elimination, in two stages, of private enterprise on the railways. In 1923 more than 100 existing railway companies were merged into the companies: LNER (London & North Eastern Railway); LMS (London Midland & Scottish Railway); GWR (Great Western Rail-

9

way); and SR (Southern Railway). By 1948, after the second world war had effectively wrecked the finances of the big four, the railways were saved only by a drastic salvage operation provided by nationalisation.

Since then, British Railways has tried to cut losses and maintain efficiency by the phasing out of steam haulage, and the 'rationalisation' of the railway system. This has entailed the closure of thousands of miles of those rural lines whose only justification for existence had been their place in a competitive network, with privately-owned railways vying with each other to bring the most attractive and convenient service to their customers.

Between 1 January 1948 (nationalisation) and 31 December 1968, more than 5,600 miles of railway in England and Wales were pruned, much of it under the 'Beeching Axe' in the 1960s. Closure often brought social upheaval, and many areas suffered economic damage. Towns and villages along particular lines lost the sense of identity with the railway and each other, that they had previously enjoyed. Yet, there is no doubt that some kind of fundamental action was needed on a system where one mid-Somerset branch line was conveying before its closure an average of six passengers and ten goods wagons a day!

It is not the object of this book to discuss the why and wherefore of British Railways' rationalisation policies. Nevertheless it is a fact that the country is now threaded with literally thousands of miles of old railway routes. The question that arises, urgently needing an answer, is 'What shall we, as a nation, do with them?'

When British Railways takes the decision to close a railway, it has to obtain the permission of the Minister of Transport for the projected closure to go ahead. Services are run down, freight transferred elsewhere, staff warned of impending transfer or redundancy, and public closure notices put up, inviting the public to lodge objections. Unless these objections are successful, which is rare, on the appointed day the last train makes its final journey and the line is officially closed. Ironically, it is often these closure rites which spur members of the travelling public to complain in bitter terms about the withdrawal of a service which their own previous neglect has killed off.

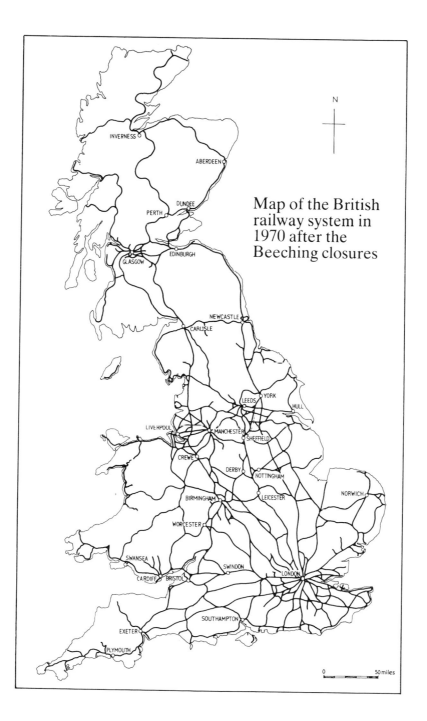

N

Map of the British
railway system in
1970 after the
Beeching closures

INVERNESS

ABERDEEN

DUNDEE
PERTH

GLASGOW EDINBURGH

NEWCASTLE
CARLISLE

LEEDS YORK
HULL
LIVERPOOL
MANCHESTER
SHEFFIELD
CREWE
DERBY
NOTTINGHAM
BIRMINGHAM
LEICESTER
NORWICH
WORCESTER

SWANSEA
SWINDON
CARDIFF BRISTOL
LONDON

SOUTHAMPTON
EXETER
PLYMOUTH

0   50 miles

Rails, sleepers and equipment are removed for use elsewhere. Bridges and viaducts may be cut down or blown up if their safety is in doubt. The track bed is then ready for purchase and use in a new role—or is abandoned and rapidly decays. A quick sale of the track bed after closure is to the advantage of British Railways; it benefits financially from the proceeds of the sale, and it passes on to the new owner the obligations peculiar to this type of land: maintenance of bridges, fencing, drainage, gates, tunnels and so on.

The usual procedure is for the land to be offered first to the relevant local authority. To quote from a government circular of 1966: 'The object (of offering the land to the local authority) is to ensure that the land in question is put to most advantageous use in the public interest as a whole'.

This has been the signal for some far-sighted authorities to seize their opportunity, and buy up old railways for conversion to footpaths and bridleways. (See Appendix A for examples.) Other authorities have balked at taking on the responsibilities of maintenance, or have failed to see the leisure possibilities of the old lines, or have simply not had the money to spare at the right time—though there are substantial grants for which authorities can apply to help with the cost of purchase and conversion. Old railways also have uses other than recreational, for example road building, refuse disposal and car parking, among many others.

If the local authority is not interested in buying the land, British Railways usually offers it to the landowners whose property abuts the line on each side. This makes it possible for the land to be converted to agricultural or other uses, but it does generally mean that sale is piecemeal, several owners perhaps being involved in a short stretch of line. This destroys the linear possibilities of the route. As far as the walker is concerned, it means that he has a large number of pieces of private property to reckon with in the course of one expedition.

If the adjacent landowners do not want to buy, the railway is then open to purchase by any interested party. Obviously the most attractive parts of an old railway are likely to be those where there are buildings in good repair, and where the land has a sideways spread. Station sites fit the bill, and these are commonly the first to be sold, and command the

The Somerset & Dorset line between Bath and Bournemouth was one of the longer routes to be closed during the 1960s. Much of the route is passable for walkers. *Above:* An enthusiast special train pulls away from Shepton Mallet in March 1966. *(John Goss). Below:* The curving Charlton viaduct at Shepton Mallet, seen here following closure after the track had been removed. *(C J F Somerville)*

highest prices. On most old lines the walker will find a good proportion of stations have been converted to private houses, with neat gardens between the platforms, and railway signs and furniture carefully restored and displayed. Considering the shape and atmosphere of many railway station rooms—bare, narrow and high-ceilinged, with small windows and a resident draught—these conversions are labours of love.

Other stations may be bought by firms for working premises. Sections of line may be bought by farmers to erect animal sheds, by coal merchants as coal dump sites, by house owners as an extension to their gardens, by contractors who want scrap metal, bricks and timber from railway construction—indeed for many different purposes.

Whichever portions of the closed line attract no offers of purchase from any source remain under the jurisdiction of the Estates Department of British Railways. This department is in theory responsible for the maintenance and care of unsold closed lines, though nature seems to work more quickly than BR, breaking down fences, filling in cuttings with undergrowth, and crumbling inexorably the abandoned station buildings.

It will soon become clear that there are three basic categories of old railway to be encountered. First, routes which have been purchased by the local authority or other body specifically for conversion to footpath or bridlepath standards. Second, those purchased or leased from British Railways by private individuals or consortia, or by local authorities for purposes other than recreational. Third, tracks which still belong to British Railways.

Where the local authority has converted the line to a public right of way, there is no problem of continuity of the route. The surface underfoot will usually be free of ballast, grass-grown or flattened; there will be no surplus undergrowth or barbed-wire obstructions. The walker can stroll on at a steady pace, free from the annoyance of blocked tunnels and bridges, or occupied station sites. He can inform himself about the history and present state of the line from introductory pamphlets prepared by the authority. He is there by right—his patronage helps to perpetuate the route. In some cases, the authority may have improved on nature by landscaping an embankment, or judicious planting of shrubs and trees. Where a portion of the line has been sold to another owner before the authority purchased the rest, a right of way will be provided around the forbidden territory. There may be picnic sites and shelters, car parks and public lavatories, information centres and helpful rangers.

This kind of old railway walking presents few problems, is a pleasure and an education to the walker, and a tribute to the perceptiveness and hard work of the authority concerned, and its employees. Appendix A contains a list of such purpose-converted lines.

Sadly (from the walker's point of view), most of the old lines in Britain fall into the second and third categories. Where private owners have bought sections of line, the subsequent use made of the track bed can be divided into two types—that bought for agricultural purposes, and that bought for other uses. A major difficulty facing the walker here is the loss of continuity. A typical two mile stretch might contain a station which has been converted into a private house, a goods shed used as a small factory, a stretch which has been ploughed up and turned into crop fields or pasture, farm sheds put up on the track, a council rubbish tip, and so on. All of these obstacles have to be negotiated one way or another by the walker.

The third category of old line—that which is still in the hands of the estates department of British Railways—is usually free of these sorts of obstructions, but may still contain broken bridges and viaducts, blocked tunnels, or cuttings choked with uncontrolled undergrowth.

In contrast to the smooth passage afforded by the first category, those in the second and third categories are definitely the rough end of the scale, where the walker is likely to pick up more scratches and stings and be wetter and muddier by the end of the day. He will also have to work much harder to unearth information about the walk, not having the benefit of ready-made pamphlets for reference. Many walkers will find consolation for the hard work and discomfort in the very solid satisfaction of breaking new ground and doing it all themselves.

Apart from the loss of continuity, the other major difficulty associated with categories two and three is the thorny problem of trespass and rights of way. Where ownership of the land is private, or where British Railways is still the owner, the walker needs permission for his expedition.

Where station buildings have been converted to private dwellings, it is a matter of commonsense and courtesy to seek the occupier's permission before going over his property. The same applies to farmland. The National Farmers' Union and British Railways have co-operated, successfully on the whole, in the conversion of old railways to farmland. To follow the route of a disused line slavishly through cornfields and young grass is to invite wrath from the long-suffering farmer.

Sadly, relationships have often been soured in the past— by landowners who look upon all ramblers as fence-breakers and crop-tramplers; and by ramblers who resent private ownership and its rights in any piece of land over which they may travel.

The sections of track still owned by British Railways present another kind of access permission problem. There is no-one actually *in situ* to grant or refuse permission. Like privately owned stretches of line, the walker would be expected to gain permission to traverse these sections—in this case from the British Railways Board (address in Appendix B). British Railways has not always dealt expeditiously with such requests, and the different regional divisions appear to hold widely differing views about ramblers.

It is to be hoped that British Railways will wake up to the fact that large numbers of people like to walk old railway lines. Obstructionist policies are potentially harmful to public relations. It is true that bureaucratic institutions tend to be cumbersome and unwieldy, and often get more than their fair share of blame for this—but it is equally true that bureaucratic institutions need a kick in the pants from time to time!

Apart from local authorities, other organisations have also taken a hand in the process of rescuing derelict railway land and preventing it from lying useless. The Countryside Commission has acted as an intermediary between local authorities and British Railways. It is a body through whose recommendation grant aid can be allowed. It also acts as a central office to whom those interested in the conversion of disused railways can apply for the relevant facts; it also provides liaison with the National Farmers' Union, the Country

16

Landowners' Association and other organisations. In May 1969 the Countryside Commission instituted the preparation of a report entitled *Disused Railways in the Countryside of England and Wales* by Dr J. H. Appleton. It is a really excellent and informative document, which anyone interested in the problem of how to use old railway networks should read. (See Bibliography.)

The Ramblers' Association, too, has been concerned with some of the schemes for conversion to footpaths, and has acted in the role of ginger group, keeping the ball rolling when it looked as if it might drop.

Local naturalists and ramblers' groups have also been concerned, and some have taken a major part in persuading the powers-that-be of the naturalistic and recreational opportunities afforded by hitherto unconsidered old lines. The reader can find out more by contacting those in his own area—or by forming such a group himself if none exists. A recently formed society is the Railway Ramblers (address in Appendix B). Its aims are:

1 To encourage interest in walking old railways.
2 To bring together small groups of ramblers to walk old railways in different parts of the country.
3 To promote conservation, clearing of undergrowth and signposting.
4 To create regional groups of Railway Ramblers.
5 To disseminate up-to-date information through news bulletins, maps, etc.
6 To alert BR and other owners of disused railway land to the growth of interest in walking old railways.

3 PREPARATION
AND RESEARCH

As every long-distance walker knows, the difference between a delightful outing and an exhausting slog is often as small as a slightly too-tight pair of boots, a sweater left behind, or a carelessly read map reference. Anyone who has read John Hillaby's fascinating account of his walk from Land's End to John O'Groats, *Journey through Britain*, will know the kind of programme that really detailed preparation can entail—weight-training, scrutiny and rejection of scores of types of footwear, painstaking research of facts about different localities, arrangements made months and hundreds of miles in advance.

Of course, the walker who is planning a stroll along his local disused branch line need not thumb his way through a library of railway information; nor need he scour the ends of the earth for the latest in nylon fibre hurricane-proof trousers. But walking old railways has its peculiar hazards and discomforts, like any other outdoor activity. There is no virtue in needlessly earning saucer-size blisters and bruises, or in walking in anything less than the maximum comfort.

By the same token, it is perfectly possible to walk 'blind' along a disused railway, simply enjoying the exercise and surroundings without knowing anything about the history of the line, or the birds and flowers one sees along the way. In the crunch of boots on ballast, rusting iron railway signs, sweeping embankments under rain-washed skies, sun on mellow brick, are subtle joys that need no explanation. But if you have unearthed enough facts to be aware that the viaduct you are approaching suffered a major collapse in building; that the station master who once presided over this broken heap of stones and brambles was famous for the marrows he grew in the station garden; that Sir John Vastly-

18

Pompous at the Hall over there between the trees held up the progress of the line through his estate for five years; that the butterfly on the rose bush is a Painted Lady; this kind of inside information adds spice to whatever you encounter on your travels. It brings in the human touch of history, the odd story, the quirky character trait, the unforeseen accident that helped to shape the finished article, and that made each railway different from its neighbour during its lifetime; and it sorts out in the walker's mind the multitude of birds, beasts and blooms that cross his path.

The walker of old railways has to be prepared for all sorts of weather, much of it unexpected, and all kinds of conditions underfoot. On a day of blazing sun and shirtsleeves, he may find himself ankle-deep in a morass at the bottom of some dank cutting—or tramping over dry ballast under a cloudy sky in mid-January. By striking a sensible balance between heat and cold, wet and dry, heavy and light, the walker can carry with him the right clothes to deal with almost all weather and conditions.

Starting from the bottom up, and at the most important end—the feet. Much has been said and written about the suitability of different types of footwear for rough walking, and every type has had its advocate, from gym shoes to heavy boots. The walker of old railways has to contend with the knobbly, ankle-turning ballast chips which, unless there is a specific agreement to the contrary, are left as 'irretrievable property' when the track is dismantled. The purchaser of the line may remove the ballast, or bulldoze it flat, if he wants to create a firm surface for vehicles or animals; but ballast is the most frequently encountered walking surface. Heavy-duty shoes with ridged or anti-slip soles are reasonably well suited to this type of walking, but with these one has no support for the ankles in the event of a stumble over rough ballast, and no protection against the smaller stones which creep between shoe and foot, causing at first discomfort, and later agony. A pair of fell-hiking boots with hard rubber soles are light, give the necessary support, and are tough enough to withstand rough going. On an old railway line whose surface has been specially restored for walkers, as on the trails and walkways, the surface is usually good enough for ordinary stout outdoor shoes.

The walker must protect his legs against the thorns and brambles that he will find everywhere on disused tracks. But there is nothing worse than sweating uncomfortably in heavy-duty trousers on a sunny day. A pair of thin jeans or corduroys strikes the right balance, and waterproof nylon over-trousers can be folded to the size of a large envelope and carried in an anorak pocket. The upper storey needs protection and comfort in equal measure too. A thin sweater can be taken off and tied round the waist by the arms and over the top a light, waterproof anorak with a zip-up front and big pockets makes for quick on-and-off changes and keeps out cold winds. A neutral colour, such as olive-green, does not advertise the walker's presence to local wildlife.

Anorak manufacturers! Why can't you make pockets in your otherwise excellent garments which are wide enough to take a standard OS map? The best method is to sling the map round the neck in a plastic map-case of the type sold in most camping shops, with a hooks-and-nylon-fur strip across the mouth which closes tightly together when pressed.

As far as other equipment goes, a pair of binoculars slung round the neck and a map of the route will suffice for a short walk. For a longer expedition, of a day's duration or more, the walker may want to take more than these basic items; nevertheless he needs equipment which is light and which does not get in the way. Festooned with heavy cameras and rolls of film, reference books and portable laboratory, he may come to feel that old railway walking is not all it is cracked up to be!

The best map for this kind of walking is the standard Ordnance Survey 1:50,000 scale (approx 1½ in–1 mile). This shows the route in surprising detail, including bridges, tunnels, embankments, cuttings and lineside buildings. Just as important, it gives the walker the shape and aspect of the surrounding countryside, and shows the relationship between towns and villages along the line. A six-inch map is fascinating to study before the walk for its wealth of minute detail, and if you can get hold of a map published before the line was closed, there is an added pleasure in seeing the railway and stations actually marked out as they were when in operation.

What no map will show you is where bridges have been cut

or viaducts dismantled, where station sites are occupied and wired off, and where cuttings have been filled with rubbish. These are things which can only be found out on the ground, and the subsequent detour has to be borne with as good a grace as possible.

Although it can be annoying to break the settled walking rhythm to check up on flora and fauna, reference books are very useful if they are small and light. A bibliography can be found at the end of the book. Notepaper, pencils, a hand-lens—these all contribute to the overall enjoyment of the walk. All this equipment can be stowed in pockets or hung on straps. If you take a back-pack, you will have to contend with the nuisance of removing it every time you need something, as well as each time you have to squeeze through brambles or wire.

So much for the walker's dress and equipment. A little research before he sets out can double his enjoyment of the walk, and one of the best places for doing this is in the cuttings section of his local public library. When a railway's closure is first proposed, it invariably stirs up discussion in the local press, letters to the Editor, nostalgic trips to Memory Junction and a host of reminiscent and indignant articles. All sorts of opinions and anecdotes, together with photographs, can be found among the newspaper clippings for the relevant years. If the cuttings go back far enough, it is often even more interesting to unearth the records of the railway's opening—step by step reports on the progress of the works, tales of the doings of the gangs of navvies, opposition from local landowners, and accounts of the opening ceremony; these were often splendidly colourful and expensive monuments to civic pride, with town bands, speeches of incredible length, banquets and balls.

For information on lines which have been converted since closure to footpaths, bridleways or linear parks, the walker can apply to the relevant organisers. For many of the trails, illustrated pamphlets and leaflets have been produced (see Appendix A).

A final, vital piece of planning that becomes second nature to the walker of old railways is to check up before departure on bus times. Most walkers will have to reach their starting-off point by car. Arrived at journey's end, the walker must return to reclaim his vehicle; but only a real stalwart will want to retrace the weary way he has come. Those Beeching-era railway users who consoled themselves for the loss of their local branch line in the expectation of a cheap, frequent and convenient country bus service have learned a hard lesson. Few and far between are the places that have gained a bus service which comes anywhere near the frequency or the speed of the railway service it has replaced. How bitter are the grindings of the teeth of the unwary, as the rear light of the last bus recedes into the gloom of a cold and rainy night, miles from anywhere! But don't rely on the lugubrious, head-shaking prophets of doom so common in pubs along the line, who say, 'Buses? Buses? Out here? You must be joking!' Ring up before you start, and save yourself a lot of bother.

4 ON THE WAY

The route is plotted; the research is done; necessary permission is sought and granted; bus times are worked out; your boots are on. As you stand on the track at the beginning of your walk, you have several miles of fascinating old railway in front of you. For the purposes of this chapter, your route lies not along a converted line, but through the rougher surroundings of virgin territory. Outlined here are a few of the problems and obstructions you may meet along the way—none insurmountable, but each needing consideration.

When a line is closed, and the maintenance gangs no longer have to make regular visits of inspection, certain constructions fall prey to wind, weather and vegetation. Most important, from a safety point of view, are bridges, viaducts and tunnels. In many cases, a major factor in the decision to close a line is the heavy expenditure required for the upkeep of these structures. After closure, responsibility for their maintenance usually passes on sale to the new owner, or stays with British Railways where the line is not sold. In general, BR has better facilities for maintenance than private owners, but in both cases the responsibility is an unrewarding burden which is not always adequately shouldered. Bricks and mortar are prized apart by weeds; rain dissolves cement and rots woodwork as it trickles down.

For this sound financial reason, British Railways very often arranges to have disused bridges and viaducts blown up or pulled down when their future safety is suspect. The scrap value of steel bridges is high, and they are rarely allowed to survive closure by many months. This widespread destruction means that the walker's journey can be interrupted at road or river—the river obviously being the bigger nuisance. Strolling along the trackbed towards a river, he finds only the stone piers of the dismantled bridge sticking up out of the water in monolithic isolation. The map gives no hint in advance, either. Jumping from pier to pier is not for those who value their necks. Improvisation is the order of the day—a nearby footbridge if you are in luck, a longer by-pass if not. Where you are planning a walk on a track which follows the line of a river valley (many of the most beautiful branch lines do), it is worth checking the map carefully before you start to see how often railway and river coincide, and working out linking routes that avoid the bridges.

Where bridges and viaducts have not been dismantled, the walker may find a tangle of barbed-wire blocking his way. These unsightly and vicious webs are often more dangerous than the bridges they guard. But on high or unsteady viaducts they are there to save the walker from a fatal plunge, and the owner from legal liability. Old railways are not dangerous places for anyone with common sense, but it is as well to steer clear of those parts which contain obvious hazards.

Tunnels also present a maintenance problem after closure. Some have been bought for various uses, among them, dumps for offensive or dangerous waste, and for mushroom growing. Their cool darkness is ideal for this activity, though some growers have found that disease spores can spread quickly from one end of a crop to the other, carried on the powerful draughts created through tunnels. In the majority of cases, tunnels are left unblocked. The danger to the walker of falling masonry, though, is plain.

When a farmer buys up disused track, it is often with the idea of putting up animal sheds and other buildings. Herds of cows and pigs are turned onto the track and fenced in at each end of the farmer's property. It is all too easy to slip under the wire and carry on along the track past animals and buildings, but this kind of intrusion will earn no thanks from the owner. The farmer may also have introduced a bull on to the line—the ultimate deterrent.

Chapter 2 notes the conversion of railway land to farm land, but local authorities, too, buy up old track with other ideas than recreation in mind. Cuttings make good sites for rubbish tips, having a ready-made hard base and sides. Some of these council rubbish tips are mountainous, spreading sideways to engulf more than just the disused track, and containing a revolting assortment of refuse. Anywhere within reach of the sea, black-backed and common gulls flock to feed on man's leavings in the company of crows and starlings. Several thousands of these scavengers, leaping into the air with raucous cries in simultaneous frenzy, beat restlessly round overhead, waiting for the intrusive walker to get on. Rats and occasionally foxes are drawn to the free feed as well—surely this is an inefficient way to get rid of hundreds of tons of rubbish, and unhealthy too. For every yard so desecrated, the old railway tracks offer many miles of walking absolutely, and in these days unusually, free of litter. However, such giant municipal dustbins do exist, and deserve a very wide berth.

One potential use for old railways which has been exploited in many places is to incorporate them into road improvement schemes. Where a road cuts across the track at right angles, problems of passage are few. Elsewhere the walker may find that what is marked clearly on his map as 'Cse of old Rly' has become part of a new main road since the map was published. Railway builders usually tried to bring their line as close as possible to towns without actually incurring the expense and upheaval of penetrating the built-up areas. The lines therefore tend to skirt round the towns, and are convenient foundations on which to base a by-pass. This can create an unexpected obstacle, as can a station site which has been bought privately and occupied, or where a new housing estate stretches across the line. There is certainly a case for asking the owner's permission to cross this kind of private land. But permission is quite likely, justifiably, to be refused—a problem which has been encountered many times by organisations trying to set up public rights of way on lines which have already been sold in part. Many are the ingenious rights of way, linking other footpaths in the vicinity, established to take the walker around these stumbling blocks: but on unconverted lines he must work it out for himself.

In places, the line of the track may have become so faint as to be indecipherable. This is particularly common in low-lying countryside and other places where the railway originally ran on the same level as the adjacent land, and subsequent years have wiped out the separate track formation. In this situation, the walker can often find his way by looking for the concrete fence-posts which bounded the railway on

Major problems often face walkers at bridges or tunnels. *Above:* Bridges and embankments have been demolished, as here on the former Kingsbridge branch. *(G M Kichenside) Left:* Waterrow Viaduct on the former Great Western Taunton–Barnstaple line. *(E A Gibbs)* Birmingham Snow Hill–*below* with trains in 1961 *(John Goss)* and *bottom right* with walkers. *(T A S Parkin)*
Top right: The former Harborne branch in Birmingham was changed out of all recognition when the cutting was filled in and grassed *(right)* in 1974/5. *(County Planning Department, West Midlands County Council)*

each side. These posts have a metal core which resists wind and rain, and keeps them upright while the surrounding cement is gradually eroded. They form a tell-tale chain of boundary markers in banks, hedges and bushes, indicating the line to be followed even when no clear indication remains on the ground. Ballast, too, resists the weather's assaults, and makes a lighter-coloured swathe in the soil which can be traced where the grass is not too thick.

At the other extreme, where sleepers and rails have been left in place, the problem is one known to anyone who has ever set foot on such a track—the disparity between the length of the human stride and the distance between the sleepers. Those walkers lucky enough to possess a stride of just the right length are in clover; the rest of us slip, slide and stumble, heel and toe, now checking and now lengthening stride—a form of progress which adds ten miles' worth of effort to a five mile walk. John Hillaby likened the exasperating motion to trying to walk rapidly on stepping-stones across a river; this was from a man who can scamper more than thirty miles a day on other, hardly less rugged surfaces. The best thing here is to admit defeat, and forsake the track in favour of the path on the outside of the rails, worn by the feet of decades of maintenance gangs, unless, that is, you can do a Blondin on the rails themselves!

The place where the line of the track is most likely to be obscured is in towns and villages. Here space is at a premium, particularly in areas of intense development. Derelict buildings and land, though surprisingly often allowed to lie unsold by BR, are liable to summary dispatch at any time after the closure of the railway. Where the walker completely loses the track in new development, he can pick up clues from the names of streets, shops, pubs and hotels—'Station Road', 'The Station Stores', 'The Railway Tavern' and so on.

The various problems and checks mentioned here are seldom frequent enough to spoil an old railway walk—in fact, they tend to add spice to otherwise bland sections. The majority of the walking is done in uncluttered, clean and open countryside, the classic branch line rural setting. Improvisation on the spur of the moment and a vigilant eye on the map are equipment enough to overcome the obstructions and side detours that crop up.

5 RELICS AND REMNANTS

Walking along an old railway, one gets the feeling that British Railways and souvenir hunters between them have picked all the meat off the bones. After all, the attraction of the whole activity, apart from physical exercise, lies in the railway environment. The term 'railway' inevitably conjures up living images of trains, station buildings, signals, signboards, busy staff, milling passengers, bridges, tunnels, and the long shining parallel lines of the track itself.

These fundamental properties of the railway either do not survive closure, or after the shut-down take on the fixed, static quality of uselessness. By the time that the railway authorities have lifted the track, dismantled the signals, and stripped the stations and signalboxes of their fittings, only the bare bones of the system are left for the explorer to examine. Souvenir hunters soon remove station nameboards, gas-lamps and the rest of the paraphernalia for which the railway property board can find no further use. Yet enough meat usually remains on the skeleton to furnish a wealth of interest for the observant walker, if he looks a little further than the derelict buildings and the empty track. The colour of the paint which peels off the station fences, the blurred 'L.M.S.' stamped on a metal plate, the charred timetable of train workings dumped in a burnt-out platelayer's cabin—all hold clues to the lineage and character of the vanished line. Poke about among the bricks and timber, and you may unearth the hidden treasure of railway history.

Looking at the historical development of Britain's railways, several layers emerge, rather like an archaeological dig. The top or most recent layer is the era of British Railways, which goes back to nationalisation in 1948. Under this top BR layer comes a four-part stratum made up of the Big Four railway companies—the Great Western, Southern, London Midland

& Scottish, and London & North Eastern railways. Digging down, we break through in 1923 into a general confusion of companies, each with its own sphere of influence in its own part of the country. An archaeologist would expect to find most evidence, and the clearest, in the top or most recent layer—the BR years. But as far as the substantial structures of the railway system are concerned—tunnels, viaducts, stations and so on—they were built long before nationalisation. Nor did the Big Four contribute the vast majority, though there was extensive rebuilding and modernisation carried out between the wars. The small, moveable objects that the walker finds usually date from the top two layers, but to deal with most of the main buildings and constructions we have to go back to the latter half of the 19th century, when the building of country branch lines was in its heyday.

In the very early railway days, hundreds of railway companies built up the main trunk network, whose routes are basically the most direct and logical, and which have survived the Beeching era. After 1850, the companies which had managed to establish profitable main routes began to turn their eyes towards the smaller companies within their area. Gobbling up the small fry as their resources expanded, the big companies stamped their styles and ideas on their own territory as they strove for a favourable public image. Now that the mad rush to the big towns was virtually over, the companies settled down to guard their home ground, and link up small and isolated points. Thus was born the branch line boom, where capillaries were added to the veins and arteries already laid down.

Station buildings remaining on disused railways can be considered in the context of the companies that put them there. Sadly, many are pulled down after closure, and others crumble into heaps of rubble by themselves. But the walker will find many still standing, some occupied and restored, others waiting for time to do its demolition work.

Until the 1850s, railway buildings were individual in character, each company building in the style it considered appropriate to the area. Local styles and materials were used at the smaller stations; huge, costly and elaborate edifices at the major termini. The companies were fighting for trade in cut-throat competition, and the weakest went to the wall.

Sophisticated customers at the city centres had to be impressed, while in country areas, where the railway was a new phenomenon, the timid traveller had to be reassured by the sight of something homely and familiar.

Unfortunately, many charming and tasteful buildings created during these early years were pulled down as the larger companies took over small lines. On branch lines some of the early buildings may survive; but in the main the walker can expect to find the standardised buildings which the larger companies began to erect as they sought to impose a 'corporate image' on their own property. The railways opened up the country, and brought isolated areas within reach of foreign ideas. As the network spread outwards, it became progressively easier for brick and iron to be moved around the country and railway architects were not slow to use these new, inexpensive and convenient materials.

Some companies—particularly the Midland Railway—continued to build in local stone. The walker in Midland territory will find well-built, sturdy stations, with typical Midland diamond-pattern lattice windows. The Midland equipped many of its station buildings with intricately-carved barge-boards (the decorative wooden boards running up and down the eaves), but most have been removed immediately after closure by sharp-eyed and light-fingered home decorators.

The London, Brighton & South Coast Railway was another company to persevere with local materials. With lines running through lovely countryside, patronised by well-to-do commuters and holidaymakers, the LBSCR did its best to provide attractive stations with a strong character. In the South Downs countryside inland, flint and red brick or stone are combined effectively, as on the Chichester to Midhurst branch—small and tidy at Cocking, large and dominating at Lavant. Italianate villa-style stations are more common near the coastal resorts.

In the south west, the London & South Western Railway used local materials in its earlier stations, though the styles were less varied—granite in Cornwall, flint near the Dorset coast, often faced with rugged slabs of rock. Local flint was used by the Great Eastern in East Anglia, too, though this may have been due more to poverty than deliberate policy.

Here the walker will often find a brick or stone wall backing the platform in place of the traditional station fence.

Where local stone was particularly accessible, the smaller railway companies made good use of it, and have left us some fine examples on their disused lines. High in the bleak grey limestone Mendip Hills, the Somerset & Dorset stations fit in perfectly with their bare, windswept environment.

The Great Northern Railway main line passed through the massive brickfields near Peterborough, and the company did much to spread the gospel of standardisation in brick. As the use of local materials declined, so the design of the buildings began to conform more and more to set patterns laid down by each company. From 1860 to 1890, the larger railways built hundreds of these functional, cheap, but rather drab stations, which dot the disused railways from Padstow to Penrith and beyond. On former Great Western lines there are scores of virtually identical buildings, one-storey red brick essays in uniformity, relieved by the awnings that over-hang the platforms. The LSWR went in for plain brick two-storey station masters' houses, whose gables loomed over one-storey office buildings on the platform. The valances, or fretted boards which hung down from the edges of the plat-form awnings, with the multiplicity of their designs lent charm to these otherwise unexciting buildings. Unlike barge-boards, many valances are still in position, or can be found in broken lengths in the undergrowth round derelict stations.

London & North Western Railway standard buildings, where not of local sandstone, appear plain and austere from the outside. The company apparently felt under no obliga-tion to provide attractive stations unless compelled by competition from other lines, though accommodation was more than adequate. Refinements of detail, so dear to the Victorian heart, were sacrificed in the standard company building to the quality on which Victorians most prided themselves—solid reliability. Thus Gordon Biddle describes the stations of the NER as 'dull but substantial villa-type standard station buildings', with a bay window as a bow to the dignity of the station master. In Lancashire & Yorkshire territory, the walker will find single-storey brick or stone buildings, some in rusty-orange flaky stone, also some two-storey structures, all functional, but few dramatic or eye-catching. In this area, however, there is some excuse for the dullness, for the buildings of the railway simply reflected the general architectural standards of the surrounding towns— quickly built, unlovely industrial sprawls, with aesthetic qualities far down on the list of priorities. This reflection of local building developments was apparent on the branch lines of the North Staffordshire Railway, too, where after some attractive early efforts a long, low, single-storey brick building appeared everywhere, squat and spartan. The Great Central, with the long thin arm of its London extension down the middle of the country, built the same characteristic stations from end to end of its London main line in the last years of the century. In Scotland, individuality of detail in station design becomes more marked the further into remote countryside one goes, with local materials widely represented. Even here the standardised station design made its appearance, though Scottish country stations were quite distinct and unlike those south of the border.

In South East England, the South Eastern Railway and the London, Chatham & Dover Railway vied with each other for nearly fifty years until their joint working agreement in 1899 under the title of the South Eastern & Chatham Railways Joint Managing Committee, a splendid mouthful usually shortened to SECR. The South Eastern Railway was a pioneer of the all-wooden station building, which became popular with many of the railway companies soon after the brick and cast-iron explosion. For impoverished companies, fighting with keen rivals for clients, these easily erected buildings cut costs and saved labour. Fewer components were involved, and they could be standardised and distributed with less effort than brick buildings. Well built, as on the LNWR, wooden stations could be as long-lasting and effective as stone or brick; hastily constructed, though, they were inefficient, uncomfortable and far from weatherproof. Of the SER and the LCDR, Gordon Biddle says, '. . . their standards of building became a byword for austere inadequacy.'

Many wooden stations are still standing, often on the smaller branch lines where money was tight; if the travelling public did not like what the railway company provided, then they had to lump it. The LSWR usually tried to cheer up its wooden stations with harmonious patterns of curves and indentations in the valances round the platform awning; the NER went in for plain designs.

Of course, there are exceptions to the rule of standardisation. Lines jointly owned by two or more companies sometimes reflected the style of one of the owners all the way through their buildings, or different styles might creep in half way along—perhaps where stations were added years later to an existing system, as on the Birkenhead Joint Railway, or where two companies met in the middle, as in the case of the Dorset Central and Somerset Central Railways.

Buildings other than the main office block—waiting rooms or shelters on the opposite platform—are often demolished before a line closes, although a surviving wooden shed or even brick or stone structure may give the walker further clues as to the general layout of the station. Sometimes corrugated iron was used in conjunction with wood in these small shelters, and occasionally in the main station building, as at stations on the GWR or LSWR.

Walking an old railway in a district such as North Wales or the Cotswolds or County Durham, where the local stone forms a natural harmony with the surrounding countryside, one may well marvel at the insensitivity of railway builders as they barged into a well-balanced building system evolved over hundreds of years, and thrust their four-square brick boxes into the middle. Yet expediency was the motive force in those unselfconscious days of industry and progress. The ugly brick boxes added life and movement, new ideas and new jobs to the scene, even if they took away some of the pastoral seclusion.

The impact of the late Victorian and early Edwardian domestic revival in British architecture brought a new wave of individualism to buildings, some well-proportioned and appropriate to their environment, others unfortunate. Terracotta bricks and tiles came in, together with a widespread use of the semi-elliptical window. Though most stations had been built by this time, a good many small stone sheds and ancillary buildings were put up as the companies carried out improvements. Among the rubble of a ruinous toilet building or store-shed, shining cream, brown and red glazed bricks can often be found, and even some terra-cotta mouldings of flowers, leaves, abstract shapes or company initials if you are especially lucky.

The first world war put a stop to most station construction, and afterwards the railways had only a few more years of independent existence. In 1923 came amalgamation, and there followed the twenty-five years of the Big Four. This was the era of the country halt, thrown up on every hand as the railways desperately tried to do battle with the encroaching motor. Villages which had campaigned for years for a station, and met with off-hand refusal, suddenly found the railway willing to lend an ear. The short concrete strip platforms, often without a shelter or even proper lighting, are common features of railway walks. Their flimsy outlines have sometimes been buried so quickly by brambles that the walker can search in vain for the site of a halt which his map shows in the vicinity, having just walked through it unawares. Sometimes platform decking has crumbled more quickly than its concrete supports, so that the bare ribs of the structure stick out in a long row of lichen-encrusted right-angles, twined with ivy and bindweed. They are monuments to a battle which turned out to be the last stand of the branch line railway.

Small delights of disused stations may come the walker's way, such as the diminutive building at West Bay, Dorset, with its tall, ornate chimneys and steeply-pitched roof over local creamy stone, all delicately executed on a miniature scale. At the other extreme is a magnificent, degraded, but still striking giant like Bath Green Park, with a feast of classical detail and an intricately fretted metal canopy in front, and stately cast-iron columns and soaring arched trainshed behind.

After studying the main buildings, do not pass by the platforms without looking at their finer details. Some are edged with glazed blocks of firebrick, rounded at the outer rim and with a criss-cross tread to steady the alighting or boarding footstep. Others may be in red brick, built all of a piece with the station buildings, or be carefully laid in blocks of local stone. If the original line of railway was doubled, or if doubling was intended but never carried out, the original platform may be in local stone and the later one in standard brick, as on the Isle of Portland branch from Weymouth. On the trackside face of the platform, look for rusty pulleys and iron loops which once held signal wires or power cables.

You will be lucky indeed to see any of the original station furniture still in situ on the platform, but keep an eye open as you pass neighbouring houses! You are quite likely to spot the ball-and-spike finial from the top of a signal in use as a flowerbed decoration, or the local railway company's initials worked into the cast-iron legs of a garden bench. Station nameboards, too, are prized collectors' items. But look for the concrete posts at the back of the platform, set about ten feet apart and with either plain or finial tops, which held up the nameboard to be seen by those in the train. If you do come across the nameboard itself, a specimen with raised concrete letters or with metal letters screwed to a wooden board is likely to be older than enamelled iron.

Platform lamps of the type supported on an upright stand-ard are usually beheaded without ceremony when their usefulness is over (the domain of British Railways must be the last stronghold of the operating gas lamp). In many places the supporting columns are left in position, twisted, fluted or hexagonal, with decorative cross-trees. From the underside of the platform awning swing Sugg gas-lamps, shaped like low-crowned metal hats, with two chains hanging from a see-saw arm on top. Small enamel nameplates, in shape like a long hot-dog between two small bridge rolls, were hung here in early BR days.

The notices in a station contribute much of its charm, and a surprising number have survived closure. LADIES, GENTLEMEN, PARCELS, TICKET OFFICE, or, more grandly, BOOKING HALL, LEFT LUGGAGE, WAY OUT, and that breath of the age of gracious travel, REFRESHMENT ROOM, jut out from the wall or hang down between the lamps from the awning. Wooden doors in the building itself may still proclaim STATIONMASTER or LAMP ROOM. Station colour-schemes varied according to district and the amount of use the station had; often many years elapsed before a station was repainted, and colour schemes sometimes changed. Even under British Railways, regional schemes continued for many years but now more standardised colours are used. Sometimes new British Rail colours may have been applied to smarten up buildings, but around lamp standards and in the obscurer corners some of the original company's colour schemes may linger.

This mixture of old and new pervades all aspects of the railway, and especially the centre of activity, the station. Turning to the archaeological layers of railway history, we find on the surface the peeling posters and paintwork of recent years. But the fixtures and fittings that lie in the next layer down tell a different story. Those massive wooden cupboards and brass-handled cash drawers have nothing in common with present-day mass-produced economy furnishings; yet a few years ago they were in full use. Here is the booking clerk's high stool, straight out of a Dickensian classroom. The embossed cast-iron fireplace, the curlicued and initialled metal brackets holding up the platform awning— these are fruits of a long-vanished craftsman's Britain. The same applies even to the fireman's ten-foot coal pricker and long-handled shovel, chucked down among weeds and forgotten when the last steam engine was withdrawn from the line, though these by now completely obsolete tools may have been made since today's teenager was born. The station is not the only part of a disused railway where the walker can look for relics and remnants of history, but it certainly attracts by far the biggest proportion of objects to itself or its immediate neighbourhood.

Away from the main buildings on the platforms, weeds, ballast and undergrowth are the dominating features of the station area. Here station plans are very useful if you are prepared to go to the trouble of unearthing them from British Railways or specialist societies or libraries, and checking on the position of vanished signal boxes, trainsheds, signals and other structures. Old photographs will do, or you can just grub about for yourself.

Signalboxes complete with levers occasionally stay intact long after closure, like the Great Western box at Radstock West which guarded the now peaceful crossing on the once congested holiday road through the town. Signals, too, seem to be forgotten from time to time by the railway dismantlers— two miles away up the Mendip slopes, an LSWR lattice mast with semaphore arm still stands at Midsomer Norton.

Engine sheds are just as impressive as station buildings in

their cavernous emptiness. Small firms, especially car repairers, often take them over even when the station itself is left to rot. On nearby walls, look for notices of exhortation to drivers—DO NOT SHUNT BEYOND THIS POINT and beside one hospital wall PLEASE SHUNT QUIETLY. Locomotive inspection pits may lurk in the undergrowth on the site of a demolished engine shed—deep, rectangular cavities with steps leading down into them, into which the train crews and maintenance men descended to work on the underparts of their engine parked above the pit. If the walker keeps to clear ground, he will do himself a favour.

Station fences, made up of cast-iron poles with spiked or spear-blade heads, or of wooden wedge-headed stakes, back the platforms and sketch out the boundary of the station area. They make marvellous pergolas for the overgrown remnants of the station flowerbeds, those badges of the branch line railway. Rambling roses, geraniums, sunflowers and pansies bear long-term witness to the green fingers of porters, signalmen and station masters, often for several hundred yards in each direction.

Apart from the station sites, there are many other railway relics to be seen as the walker goes along. Such lineside buildings as platelayers' cabins are worth inspecting. Sometimes they are quite luxurious affairs, built solidly of red brick with wooden benches, plank floors and an iron firegrate—even little cupboards for the worker's tools and dinner tins. More often they are a standard concrete design, with small windows and hard floors. Others have been banged together out of old sleepers coated with tar. Many things see daylight for the first time in years as one rummages in these cramped huts: shovels with 'BR' burned into the wooden handle, old greasy pre-nationalisation timetables, or occasionally important-looking pieces of equipment. Once I found a complicated gadget loaded with springs and levers, with the mysterious legend 'Voidometer' printed across the dial. A machine for measuring blank spaces seems quite at home in a branch line platelayers' cabin.

At the site of a level crossing, the crossing-keeper's cottage is likely to be privately occupied. These well-designed though small houses were often laid out more conveniently and comfortably than the station house. Sometimes the company

Above: For much of its route the Somerset & Dorset line consists generally of a footway along the former trackbed, with little evidence that it was once a railway other than exposed patches of ballast and the occasional notice such as the one illustrated. *(C J F Somerville)*

Below: The station at Bath Green Park, northern terminus of the Somerset & Dorset line, retains its overall roof but the site has now become a local authority car park. *(C J F Somerville)*

Most station closures in major city centres have been followed by total demolition and redevelopment of the site. Unfortunately some of the superb architectural features of these major stations are usually lost for ever. This is the overall roof of Glasgow St Enoch station shortly after closure in 1966. *(John Goss)*. Ornamental station lamp posts often remain in position at smaller stations or form collectors items. *(John Goss)*

decorated them with bargeboards of the same pattern as those at the station. Often they are dated, in a concrete or terra-cotta plaque high up on the wall. Beside the cottage, the heavy white-painted level crossing gates with the big red circle in the middle and a diagonal iron rod may still be in place across the track, and the walker will have to wriggle through a kissing-gate at the side. Elsewhere the gates have just been thrown aside into the hedge. Here too the present occupier may have bought a section of track with the cottage; it is worth checking on rights of passage at the cottage door.

Where sidings run away from the main track, look by the side of the line for the large square box of the ground frame which controlled entry to the siding. Here were levers, worked by those entrusted with a key, which switched the points.

Sleepers, either wooden or concrete, are well worth inspecting whenever the walker spots one. Still bolted to them may be a heavy cast 'chair', with massive jaws into which the rail was fitted to be held tightly by a wooden or spring steel 'key'. If you find a chair, look closely at the numbers and letters stamped on each corner of the upper surface. On one corner will be the initials of the railway company on whose order the chair was made. Usually BR, occasionally GWR, LMS, SR or LNER, on rare occasions a

40

pre-grouping company's chair—perhaps an oval LBSCR, or a large square LNWR or GER. In another corner is stamped the year the chair was made, and often the abbreviation for the month as well—MAR 1932. The foundry which produced the chair—sometimes GKN—put their initials on the third corner, and a serial or type number on the fourth.

Where sleepers and rails are still in position, you can follow a whole succession of these dates, seeing when a particular section was relaid and by whom; sometimes on awkwardly placed bridges or long-disused sidings there might even be sleepers with chairs which no-one has tried to replace since the original company laid the line. Wooden sleepers last wonderfully well, as any scrap timber merchant can tell. Coated with tar and creosote, soaked in a century of engine oil, they keep out all weathers. Farmers use enormous quantities to build up new barn walls, and thcy do duty as gardcn fences, gate-posts, milk-churn stands and a thousand and one other things throughout the district. The tell-tale bolt holes through a paler square at each end where the chair used to sit, give away their origins.

GREAT NORTHERN RAILWAY
PUBLIC WARNING NOT TO TRESPASS

Persons trespassing upon any Railway belonging or leased to or worked by the Great Northern Railway Company solely or in conjunction with any other Company or Companies, are liable to a penalty of FORTY SHILLINGS under the Great Northern Railway Act 1890, and in accordance with the provisions of the said Act public warning is hereby given to all persons not to trespass upon the said Railways.

KING'S CROSS. JULY 1896   BY ORDER.

All sorts of signs and notices remain on disused railways, those for which the railway authorities have no further use and which collectors cannot unscrew, thanks to the great rivets which clamp the sign to its post. The most common are those large heavy squares of cast-iron, headed by the name of the company and signed 'BY ORDER', with the letters raised in a kind of railway Braille. Built to admonish for ever, they project their wordy, pompous warnings of 'A PENALTY OF FORTY SHILLINGS or ONE MONTH'S IMPRISONMENT' from blackberry bushes and new housing sites.

Other cast-iron notices can be found where small road bridges with weight restrictions cross over the railway. Set facing the road only a couple of feet from the bridge itself, their closely-lettered lozenge-shaped faces required the reader to absorb about twenty words a second, and to perform some complicated mental arithmetic involving unladen and laden axle-weights, as he approached. Nowadays, cars flash by unheeding; but even in the more leisurely days of horse and trap, did farmers and travellers ever actually dismount and spell over the close-packed legalistic jargon of words and figures before braving the bridge? More likely the signs were put up simply as legal cover in case of accident. One wonders whether the drivers of gigantic juggernauts realise as they thunder over hump-back bridges that the rusty sign down there is forbidding them the use of the bridge if their laden axle-weight is more than two tons!

On many of these signs can be traced the history of changing ownership of the line, as British Railways shuffled regional borders. On an LSWR sign, for instance, the L and S could be deleted to leave WR for Western Region. The Southern Region, on taking over, only had to reinstate the S and paint out the W to give themselves an appropriate sign at no extra cost; even though the actual fine mentioned might be ludicrously out of date, the heavy Victorian warning was clear enough. Sad to think that this admirable sense of economy never stretched far enough to save the railway itself.

On the boundaries of their land, the companies erected boundary markers, which often survive unscathed in hedgerows and ditches, sited away from the track itself. The Great Western favoured a round-headed type, dated and stamped 'GREAT WESTERN RAILWAY BOUNDARY'. On many branch lines the Midland used a simple iron post about two feet high, with the letters M and R separated by a spoked locomotive wheel.

Other cast-iron plaques which may have escaped collectors

can be found on bridges; usually they are oval and carry the bridge number. Iron bridges often have elaborately shaped heraldic shields riveted to their inside frame, bearing the maker's name and town and the date of construction. Many emanate from the London firm of Joseph Westwood, and still more from the Butterly Company which made a speciality of railway ironwork, including some fine columns at St Pancras which still bear the firm's signature.

Engine drivers needed big, clearly lettered signs placed at a convenient angle to the track. Look for the long 'WHISTLE' notices by level crossings, in black with white lettering; also the cryptic 'SW' by bridges, sharp curves, tunnels and stations, which stands for whistle. Another kind of sign for the benefit of engine crews was the gradient marker, usually a low concrete post with arms. The angle of the arms up or down, and the figures moulded on them, showed the rate of climb or fall. They can often still be found, sometimes armless, among trackside brambles.

The railways, keen to emphasise their sovereignty over their patch, were wont to spray their initials around the general area of the railway line like confetti. Gateways that give onto the track may have a signed post or hinges—even fence posts in fields well away from the line bear initials and dates in some places. Where stations are sited in towns, especially at the terminus, the company hotel or railway pub may have a sign painted with a scene from the railway past, relics, and locals with long memories in the bar.

Below all the buildings and furniture, the fixtures and fittings, lies the very bedrock of the railway—the bridges and tunnels, embankments and cuttings, and the tenacious scar of the trackbed itself. These foundations, the first to be laid, are also the last to vanish. Those bridges which have not been destroyed may be in company brick, or local stone where it was easily quarried. Even where the face of a bridge presents a rugged, rough-hewn aspect, there is likely to be prosaic red brick behind. Rustic facings were popular with all the companies on bridges and viaducts, sometimes completely concealing the underlying brick, sometimes in a curious 'half-faced' style. The workmanship in bridges built on a slant or at an angle is to be admired; also the attention to detail that saw the smallest cattle-bridge or culvert carefully faced and topped with shaped stone blocks. On the arch of an overbridge or tunnel mouth you might see a spreading black stain where thick smoke from locomotive chimneys blasted upwards, crusting the bricks with soot. Where the bridge is built on steeply-sloping track which was once double, compare the smoke stains on each side of the bridge. On the side where the engines passed under the bridge climbing hard, the stain is twice as heavy and concentrated as on the other side, where the drivers going in the opposite direction had shut off steam and were coasting down the bank.

Pedestrian over-bridges may be made of wood, some intricately balustraded and scalloped, others just a plank span. Iron lattice-girder bridges, carrying the railway across water, are agreeable to look at, a striking blend of strength and subtlety—but their value as scrap means that there are few left in position.

Viaducts, of course, have a gigantic beauty which has been the making of many an uninspiring valley view. The sympathetic and detailed works of the 19th century lithographer J. C. Bourne have captured perfectly the mixture of grandeur and sweated labour in their building. Like bridges, some viaducts are formed of tall stone, brick, or later reinforced concrete arches. Others are like extended lattice-girder bridges, supported on stone piers.

I have touched on tunnels in an earlier chapter. If you do not mind walking through their dark, smoke-perfumed chambers, look for the recessed niches set at intervals in the tunnel wall into which the maintenance men had to press themselves when caught by a train in the tunnel. Stalactites form on the tunnel roof, especially in limestone country. Green algae thrive on the cakes of nutritious soot that cling to the walls near the tunnel mouth.

Money was tight on the small branch lines. To avoid the enormous expense and delay of tunnelling and viaduct building, the railway would snake in tortuous curves, following contour lines, hugging hillsides and valley floors, utilising old tramways and dried-up canal beds. In spite of this, however, a good deal of embankment building and cutting excavation was always necessary; and even in the flattest countryside the trackbed needed thousands upon thousands of barrow-loads of earth foundations and ballast stones. Here is a fitting place to pay tribute to the men whose muscles actually built the railways—the navvies. These itinerant labourers, universally feared and held in abhorrence, tramped from job to job, staying with the line until it was built or until they heard of higher wages elsewhere. Exploited, enslaved by 'beer-on-the-job' and payment in truck tickets which could only be redeemed against over-priced goods at the contractors' own tommy shops, they worked their guts out with pick and barrow. They lived in miserable encampments by the line, building their own huts out of whatever materials lay at hand—stones, scrap wood or even sods of turf. They accomplished feats of earth-moving, mounding, digging and blasting which had never been seen before. They drank themselves stupid on the works and in the pubs, marched in internecine strife, took appalling risks on the job to save a few minutes, and died in large numbers of accident and disease. Some of the contractors tried to soften their lot with more or less effective welfare schemes—a doctor, a priest, some handouts of clothes or food; most didn't give a damn as long as the work went ahead to schedule. The navvies' names were like nothing that had been seen before, either—Dolly-legged Punch, Shadow and Bones, Starch-'em-Stiff and Scandalous. When they died, the mourners were few. But the death of two navvies on the Ely to Peterborough line on Christmas Eve 1845 occasioned this marvellous poetic epitaph, inscribed on a tombstone at Ely Cathedral:

THE SPIRITUAL RAILWAY

The line to Heaven by Christ was made
With heavenly truth the rails are laid
From Earth to Heaven the Line extends
To Life Eternal where it ends

Repentance is the Station then
Where Passengers are taken in
No Fee for them is there to pay
For Jesus is himself the way

God's Word is the first Engineer
It points the way to Heaven so clear,
Through tunnels dark and dreary here
It does the way to Glory steer

God's Love the Fire, his Truth the Steam,
Which drives the Engine and the Train
All you who would to Glory ride,
Must come to Christ, in him abide

In First and Second, and Third Class,
Repentance, Faith and Holiness
You must the way to Glory gain
Or you with Christ will not remain

Come then poor Sinners, now's the time
At any Station on the Line
If you'll repent and turn from Sin
The train will stop and take you in

The navvies built the railways and passed on unlamented. Yet in countless cuttings they have left their marks for the walker to see, the scratches of the pick-axe heads in hard rock, and the small round shot-holes where the blasting powder was packed; and every embankment heaped up speaks eloquently of their energy and capacity for hard work and stoic endurance. The sheer physical effort required to cut a passage thirty feet deep through two miles of rock is almost beyond belief; yet these men managed it, and got fighting drunk afterwards.

This chaper has touched in a general way on some of the remnants to be found on a disused railway, but sharp eyes and a willingness to poke around will do most to unearth the treasures of railway history.

6 FLORA AND FAUNA

One of the principal joys of walking old railway lines lies in observing nature fighting for a living in a severely man-polluted environment. Nature is wonderfully resilient, in spite of the beating she has to take from our technological society. The building of motorways to siphon off heavy traffic from the overburdened main roads has often been followed by a gradual restocking of wildlife and plants along the verges of those earlier roads, depleted of their share of plants and animals through many years' accumulation of filth and the prolonged effects of fumes.

Some plants and animals manage to co-exist with operating railways—witness the long purple banks of rosebay willow-herb to be glimpsed out of any carriage window on any line in the country. But when smoke and cinders, or, nowadays, diesel smuts, have gone, and the cuttings and embankments have fallen into the silence of abandonment, the closed lines provide ideal refuge for many kinds of birds, beasts and plants.

When a line closes and the rails and sleepers are lifted, the dirty, bitter ballast stones which are exposed repel almost all plant life at first. Slowly the flat creeping plants sidle in from the verges and establish a toe-hold. The aromatic purple flowers of ground ivy with a matted tangle of runners appear on the trackbed, and in damp cuttings you may find the five pale yellow petals and silvery-green toothed leaves of silver-weed. Yellow coltsfoot grows on the track, too, and sticky cleavers twine round bramble bushes, waiting to hitch a ride on your trouser-leg to their reproductive destiny.

Short plants come next in the regenerative process—purple creeping thistle, yellow groundsel and white chickweed spread their small flowers across the ballast. Look for the fine branched leaves and stubby, rounded yellow flowerheads of the fragrant and aptly-named pineapple mayweed.

When the short plants are established, medium-sized plants (one to two feet tall) make their appearance. Toadflax is seen widely in summer, the flowers showing a conspicuous orange spot on a pale yellow petal. In late spring, the straight stems of goatsbeard stand stiffly up out of the trackbed, the crowded yellow flowerhead cupped in long green spiky fingers. It needs a sunny day to see this plant fully open, and even then you must find it before midday; in cloudy weather—and in the afternoon, cloudy or sunny—the spiky bracts close up around the flower, and the goatsbeard reveals the origin of its folk name 'Jack-go-to-bed-at-noon'.

The tall flowers (over two feet) are, surprisingly, often not the ones which the walker notices first. Mulleins are fairly common on bare, dry and waste ground; they are a tall, sturdy family, with yellowish, small flowers running in alternation up a spear-blade shaped head. The great mullein, with its broad five-leaved flowers and overall coating of thick white wool, is a very impressive plant.

Related to the mulleins, but more commonplace to look at, is figwort. This is another plant which likes the shadier places, and is most likely to be found in a cool cutting, or where trees hang closely over the track. Ragwort, like a more robust version of groundsel, grows directly on the track where grass has taken over from naked ballast. Bushy pink hemp agrimony, on a tough red stalk, is another plant that thrives in the harsh waste-ground environment. Frequently seen is smooth sowthistle, with yellow dandelion heads, big

Rosebay Willowherb and Couch Grass

ragged pale-green leaves, and a stem which exudes an acrid milky gum when crushed. Giant woolly thistles nod and bob in summer under the weight of foraging bees.

After, or in many cases instead of, the tall flowering plants come brambles and thorns, and lastly the shrub bushes and tree suckers: hazel bushes, slim-leaved willow, heavy with powdery catkins in spring, holly bushes and young elder, blackthorn, with delicate white flowers and a fiendish jab for the careless passer-by, and many others. These dense bushes grow unchecked on the unconverted lines, flourishing in the damp, badly-drained cuttings, and often reaching a height well in excess of 20 ft. Where they have really taken hold, on a line which has been closed for a quarter of a century, for example, it is quicker, and less agonising, to make a detour.

The variety of flora that grow on the trackbed itself is affected by the kind of ballast that was used in the building of the line—limestone, shale, cinders, ash and so on—and by whether the track has been left undisturbed since closure. The builders of the Buxton to Ashbourne line in Derbyshire made use of local limestone for ballast. When the Peak Park Planning Board developed the Tissington Trail along this line, they disguised the white scar of the trackbed across the landscape and improved the walking surface by covering the limestone ballast with four inches of soil and seeding with grass. Subsequent heavy use by horse riders badly churned up the grass, and the Trail was resurfaced with finely crushed dark-coloured waste basalt. Waste basalt was also used to resurface the Peak Park Planning Board's neighbouring High Peak Trail, which is based on the track of the Cromford & High Peak Railway. On this line, the ballast was mostly of ash, with coarse limestone used on the Northern section. These different types of surface give rise to a wide variety of habitat for plants in a small area. The whole district is rich in flowers typical of limestone soils, and five areas along the line are managed as nature reserves by the Derbyshire Naturalist Trust.

Away from the trackbed, embankment and cutting sides provide more of a refuge for plants. Primroses and cowslips, those survivors of a vanished pastoral age, have forsaken the once isolated but now desecrated meadows for the seclusion of disused railways, often joined by brightly coloured primulas which have exchanged the pampered earth of their native gardens for the rugged wild. A survey carried out on a railway embankment at Beighton, on the borders of Derbyshire and South Yorkshire, indicates the large variety of plant species attracted to this kind of environment. Although the site of the survey is only a few miles northeast of the High Peak and Tissington Trails, the soil here is of shale mixed with clay. An area of 50 by 10 yd was surveyed, and within this rectangle the researcher found thirty-seven plant species. They included four kinds of grasses, soft rush and horsetail, pussy willow, broom and gorse as well as numerous flowers such as tansy, groundsel, yarrow, mugwort, and almost inevitably rosebay willowherb. Another flower found in profusion in this survey was Oxford ragwort, an introduced cousin of groundsel which has spread very quickly in the railway environment in recent years.

Similar types of survey have been carried out by local naturalist societies all over Britain, on disused lines and on lines still functioning. The potential of old railways as refuges for wildlife in an increasingly man-dominated and hostile world has been noticed by those local authorities with an eye to the conversion of disused lines to footpaths and bridleways. When conversion schemes are discussed, the abandoned railways are put under the microscope, probably for the first time since their closure. In Lincolnshire, for example, a report produced in 1970 by the then Lindsey County Council laid great stress on the importance of the derelict tracks as providers of undisturbed habitat, an importance which increases year by year as arable farming is intensified in the flat eastern countryside. Here, where hedges have been grubbed out, elder and willow cut down and heathland put under the plough, the old railways, strips of man-made environment that they are, have assumed a naturalistic status which those concerned with local wildlife are determined not to neglect. The 'Spa Trail' has already been established on the Woodhall Junction—Horncastle line, which passes through heathland and coniferous woodland. The Louth—Firsby Junction line covers grassland, scrub and woodland, while the old track from Woodhall Junction to Bellwater Junction passes a series of flooded gravel pits which have been designated sites of special scientific interest, with fishing, water birds, marine life, and a process of planned replanting and natural regeneration taking place simultaneously. Sadly, the Louth—Firsby and Woodhall—Bellwater lines have not yet been officially converted.

This vital function of old railways as preservers of natural habitat has been meticulously documented by the botany department of Aberdeen University in a survey of wildlife on the disused Deeside line, which contains at each end of its forty-two mile length a type of environment quite distinct from the rest of the line, both rich in wildlife.

At the eastern end of the line, the survey concentrated on a short stretch from Cults, near Aberdeen, to Peterculter, by an intensive study of about two and a half acres. Roughly 150 plant species were found in this area, a surprisingly high number in a well-populated, semi-suburban region. Such short-lived plants as sticky groundsel and ivy-leaved toadflax inhabit the track margins. Sycamore, ash, beech, cherry and wych elm, scrub birch and willow, raspberries and brambles have all appeared, with gorse, broom, snowberry and dog roses colonising the more open places. Garden escapes have arrived, too—Solomon's seal, buddleia and toadflax. On the damp walls of the station buildings the researchers found ferns flourishing, including some which are rare in lowland areas—black spleenwort, maidenhair spleenwort, wall-rue and bladder fern.

This section of the line is used heavily by people wanting a short walk out from Aberdeen. The report recommends future action which could be taken to enhance the value of the path. This includes selective weeding and cutting back to preserve attractive views and to allow plants to survive, and some suggestions for plants which might be introduced to grow quickly, look agreeable, and increase the diversity and interest of the plant life (and animal life, in the shape of butterflies and birds), with trees, flowering shrubs and plots of gregarious flowers as ground cover. In an area where many people use the line, a balance between natural and introduced hardy plants makes for an attractive footpath, and one whose attractions can withstand such heavy use.

The other section studied by the researchers lay at the western end of the line, more than thirty miles away. The land is higher, wilder and more isolated here. Where the railway passed through birch scrub and coniferous woodland, it has had the effect of enriching the local flora by virtue of the improved drainage it has brought to the acid grassland or heath. Birch, alder and larch grow in these parts, and the damp walls of cuttings support several kinds of mosses and ferns. Further on, the line straightens out and passes through farmland on both sides. Here the soil is alluvial, and the vegetation is enticingly described in the report as having 'the character of a herb rich meadow'. Taller plants, such as sweet cicely, hogweed and black knapweed grow on the verges of the track.

The researchers advised a few introductions here as well, though not as many as at the 'popular' end near Aberdeen. Wild cherry, rowan and holly would mix with the neighbouring woodland. In the more agricultural section, the report recommended the planting of a 'herb-rich hedge', partly to give refuge to birds and animals, partly to break up the views of the approaching Grampian mountains. This suggestion has particular relevance in a Britain where ancient hedges, some well over a thousand years old, have been levelled and destroyed to create bigger fields.

In the two short stretches of line covered by the researchers, ten butterfly species were noted—common blue, meadow brown, large white, small white, green-veined white, small tortoiseshell, small copper, grayling, red admiral and painted lady. Among twenty-eight bird species seen were greenfinch, willow warbler, black-headed gull, lesser redpoll, whitethroat, blackcap, chaffinch and goldcrest. The plant list really brings home the importance of this old railway as a storehouse of nature, for no fewer than 249 species were recorded. They included twenty-nine grasses, sedges and rushes, eleven types of fern, more than thirty mosses and liverworts, and many lichens, nineteen tree and eleven shrub species, and scores of flowers of all descriptions. You could even lunch off domestic escapes—strawberries, raspberries, gooseberries and potatoes.

The process of replanting old railway walks has to be undertaken on a more formal basis where the line runs in a built-up area. The whole layout has to be rigidly planned and adhered to, taking into account the very heavy use, the problems of pollution and rubbish accumulation, and the likelihood of vandalism. In this kind of environment plants which were indigenous to the line before its closure are less likely to have survived than in the isolated and less rapidly changing environment of the countryside. In big cities these problems are aggravated by the lack of sideways space, and by pressure from housing and industrial concerns over the use of derelict land.

In spite of the difficulties, a number of short walks have been created on lines in cities, the most notable of which has been the 'greenway' system built up in the heart of Stoke-on-Trent (see Chapter 12 and Appendix A). The types of plants chosen by the London Borough of Haringey for two schemes currently in hand are typical of the attractive but tough shrubs, trees and flowering plants which have a good chance of survival. At Muswell Hill, the short walk is to be planted with silver birch, Norway maple, alder, great sallow and hawthorn; low shrub cover is made up of common gorse, dwarf gorse and various brambles; virginia creeper and ivy are trained along the fences on each side of the track. At Park Avenue to the north, there is a disused cutting to be replanted. Here the walker sees bushes of gorse, roses and Japanese bamboo as he descends onto the track. Groups of trees similar to those at Muswell Hill are set on each side of a winding path, with shrubs on each bank including elder, cotoneaster, sea buckthorn and barberry. At the other end of the cutting, the walker climbs up to street level between bushes of ivy, cherry laurel and Spanish broom. These plants are common to city parks and public spaces, and although better than dereliction will inevitably have the effect of replacing the old railway atmosphere with a more formal 'public gardens' setting. But Haringey Borough Council has another scheme in preparation, planned jointly with Islington Borough Council. This is for a parkland walk from Highgate to Finsbury Park, a biological corridor established through two miles of London, less formally laid out than the two schemes mentioned above and with more chance for natural regeneration to take place. At Brinnington in Stockport, Greater Manchester, there is a greater amount of linear space available, and here some hedge planting is planned, mainly of thorn, with wild rose, elder and holly.

As well as being the scene of natural and artificial regeneration, old railway tracks are nowadays being pressed into service as participants in the funeral rites of the many thousands of elm trees stricken fatally with Dutch elm disease. These elephants' graveyards are usually in cuttings, which a contractor fills with the enormous carcasses of felled elms, waiting for the knacker's lorry.

Beside the flowering plants, there are other attractions growing on and around old railways. Fungi of all shapes and sizes sprout from rotten trees and wood fences. The lineside trees often bear a good coat of lichen, a sure sign of unpolluted air—especially Usnea, the thick grey-green 'old man's beard' of lichens which cannot live under any except the purest air conditions.

The wide variety of plants on old railways are used for food and shelter by many kinds of insects, which themselves attract a multitude of birds. At ground level, emerald and brown beetles—occasionally a stag beetle, carrying his antlers with jerky movements across a rotten sleeper or log. Clumps of wild buddleia and dog-roses attract bees in summer. The electric green and blue aerial daggers of dragonflies skim and hover where the line runs near water. Butterflies converge on unfrequented tracks. Tortoiseshells, peacocks and red admirals can be seen in many places, and other varieties include the common blue, the startlingly bright yellow brimstone, orange-tip, chunky brown skippers, and the gleaming black and crimson wings of the six-spot burnet moth. At Lyncombe Vale near Bath, on the track of the Somerset & Dorset Railway, the white-letter hairstreak is quite a frequent visitor. It is a lovely butterfly, with a row of white dots down each side of the wings and a wavy red stripe on the trailing wing. Spiders do the walker a favour, getting rid of large numbers of his chief tormentors, the thrice-damned neck-biting flies.

In any environment, bird life is dependent for its variety on the type of cover and food supply available. Among the bushes and scrub of the deserted railway lines, many species which in other circumstances are shy and hard to find can be seen. Along the track, long-tailed tits swing like trapeze artistes in the bushes, for they like the taller hazel thickets, as do goldcrests. In fact, the two are often seen together.

Larks ascend tunefully from trackside tufts of grass. Thrushes abound on old railway lines; slugs and snails are attracted to cool damp cuttings and the brickwork of tunnel mouths and bridge abutments, and these places make good hunting haunts for the rapacious thrush.

Magpies and jays clatter off, screeching out their general alarms. Green woodpeckers swoop up and down as they fly directly ahead of the walker, often covering several hundred yards in a teasing game of catch-me-if-you-can before swerving abruptly aside into cover. Their black and white speckled cousins, the red-headed greater spotted woodpeckers, are frequently seen where the trackside woodland has a high proportion of coniferous trees. Watch out for heart attacks when walking through autumnal woods—partridges and pheasants seek out old railway lines for safety in the shooting season, and shatter the nerves of the unsuspecting walker as they burst explosively from the cover of leaves or bushes.

Herons are often to be seen in marshy places, while overhead tumble lapwings, the clown princes of aerobatics. They add a dash of rogue humour to a springtime walk as they fall like bundles of black and white rags, seemingly out of control, only to recover acrobatically and fly clumsily away a few inches from the ground. Hawks are another feature of old railway walks. The kitten's mew cry of the buzzard often heralds a sight of the bird itself, drifting overhead on broad outstretched wings. Kestrels and sparrowhawks, slim and deadly, speed across the track at hedge-top height in search of prey, or hover with trembling, tapered wings and head tucked down between shoulders, scanning the ground with telescopic eyes.

Aquatic life is not so easily seen, of course. Newts and frogs may be found when drainage ditches have overflowed to form ponds. For the most part, the walker will have to make a special detour to a marl hole, gravel pit or pond nearby, either one that he happens across, or on converted lines a pool stocked and maintained specifically for the study and culture of aquatic forms of life. Typical of these is the proposal set out in the Preliminary Report of the Bath City Architect and Planning Officer concerning the stream in the Lyncombe Vale nature trail area of the Somerset & Dorset Railway track.

'. . . it is considered that the stream should be exploited in some manner. As any form of over-exploitation would endanger the natural succession and regeneration processes, it is proposed to create a unit for the study of a fresh water ecology. This would be in strict keeping with the function of the remainder of this section and should, again with some form of control, not endanger the natural processes.

The fresh water ecology study unit would be created by forming a pond on part of the area that is at present derelict allotment. The unit would be so constructed as to provide as many differing types of fresh water habitat as possible, eg fast moving water, slow moving water, stagnant water, etc. This can be achieved by the construction of varying depths of pool, dams, spillways, etc. Provision would have to be made for some form of jetty or platform to allow study to be carried out from the centre of the pond as well as from the edges.'

Wild animals enjoy freedom from noise and pollution on old lines, and tend to suspend their habitual distrust of the approaching human figure. Rabbits, hares and foxes, so difficult to observe at close quarters, are less quick to connect the outlines of the human with danger.

Badger setts are on the increase, too, though a sight of the badger himself will be a rare treat as old railway lines are not safe places to walk along at night. However, given access to the line at a point near to the sett, an evening's static badger-watching should be very profitable in such a quiet and unfrequented environment. In forested areas of Scotland, pine martens have been habitual users of old railways; wild cats, too, have been recorded, though as usual it is difficult to say with certainty whether the genuine *felis sylvestris* has been sighted, or just *felis domesticus* on a camping holiday.

Not all wildlife sightings bring pleasure. On the high Cotswold line between Andoversford and Cirencester, I noticed at a certain point a peculiar smell, getting stronger as I walked. I looked round for sewage farms or dead animals, but could see nothing. Then a movement in the hedgerow attracted my eye—the swaying of a row of shrunken, shrivelled bodies on a wire. The once sleek brown fur of the weasels was matted and bloody, and the stoats which hung among them stared grotesquely out of blank eye sockets, picked clean by the birds. A truly disgusting testimony to some gamekeeper's zeal.

On one walk I found a striking death tableau by the side of the Taunton—Barnstaple line. At first sight it looked like a large fungus, but on going closer to inspect, I found a dead hedgehog, its mottled spines erect, clamped in a relentless grip round the half-denuded skeleton of a stoat, the white bony jaws wide open in a rictus of effort. Here was the aftermath of an epic, unseen battle fought out between the suave, tapering killer and its placid, spiky opponent—a scene straight out of Henry Williamson. After many snarling manoeuvres the fight ended with the hedgehog, its neck bitten through, taking revenge with a grip so powerful that the stoat was unable to get away, and died days later of starvation.

A hand lens for the plants and insects and a pair of binoculars for the animals and birds—plus the appropriate pocket guides—are all the equipment the walker need take with him. If he is planning a walk along a converted line, the pamphlets and booklets produced by the organisers are usually well worth the few pence they may cost, though many are free. The Wirral Country Park booklets mentioned in Chapter 10 are superbly informative and so are those produced for the High Peak and Tissington Trails. The pamphlets for the 'Waters of Leith' walkway near Edinburgh go into great detail about the effect on plant and animal life of sun, shade, soil acidity, water erosion and other natural phenomena. Many other organisations, and particularly the country parks, have taken great trouble to inform their visitors about resident wildlife.

For specific information about an unconverted line, the local botanical, ornithological or naturalist societies may have produced their findings in printed form. It is worthwhile contacting them in any case to find out what kind of work they have done relating to the line. These societies often work closely with the organisers of converted lines, submitting their records to the general information collection or taking on responsibility for one aspect of wildlife preservation.

Ecology, or the interaction of the different parts of nature, is the watch-word of our age. With their rich variety of habitat and their solitude, old railways have an immensely important part to play as ecological oases in a technological desert. The city planner who condemns a strip of track out of hand as 'useless' and builds over it, the farmer who allows his pesticides to poison the old line through his property, the local authority which only sees the derelict cutting as a potential rubbish tip, are all recklessly throwing away a valuable resource. The walker has his part to play, too: every flower picked, every cigarette packet thrown down upsets the balance which nature creates. By keeping to his path and observing the 'look; don't touch' rule, the walker preserves the environment he has come to enjoy, and makes sure that those who follow him are not seen as enemies by either wildlife or farmers. The Country Code is usually added at the end of outdoor books, like an afterthought; I make no apology for concluding this chapter with it.

THE COUNTRY CODE

*GUARD AGAINST ALL RISK OF FIRE
*FASTEN ALL GATES
*KEEP DOGS UNDER PROPER CONTROL
*KEEP TO THE PATHS ACROSS FARMLAND
*AVOID DAMAGING FENCES, HEDGES AND WALLS
*LEAVE NO LITTER
*SAFEGUARD WATER SUPPLIES
*PROTECT WILD LIFE, WILD PLANTS AND TREES
*GO CAREFULLY ON COUNTRY ROADS
*RESPECT THE LIFE OF THE COUNTRYSIDE

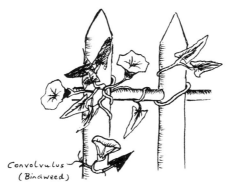

Convolvulus
(Bindweed)

7 SOME VIEWS

Judging by the graffiti scribbled over the closure notices at Toller Porcorum station, it had been the same old story. Here was a typical country branch line deep in Hardy's Wessex, connecting the town of Maiden Newton with the small seaside resort of Bridport, ignored for years by the travellers whose patronage might have helped it to survive. Now it was closed, and indignation reigned.

TOLLER 1975—THE END OF AN ERA

In loving memory of the Bridport Branch. May you rest in peace. Love Toller and Powerstock.

Must everything be governed by finance?

ARE WE ALL MAD?—£500 million poured out to save jobs of Leyland workers.

Another Nail in the coffin of British Railways!

And yet another thing of charm and quality taken from the Modern Age.

Come and live in Britain, the country that cares about you! £1,000,000 millions spent on Concorde but we can't afford a mere £50,000 to retain our vital rural links.

When a disused railway runs into towns and villages, there is interest of a different kind from the open countryside. The walker has the opportunity of seeing the generally unseen side of such places—factory back yards, sewage farms loud with gulls, and waterworks; the goods entrances of shops, the shabby, small-windowed and heavily drainpiped backs of premises which present a bright, smiling image to the High Street. Old advertisements for long-forgotten products can be deciphered, painted high up on the dark side of walls:

'JO   SON'S FIN ST MPIRE T BACC '

From this angle one gets clues to the past functions of buildings. Here is a pressing-stone from a cider-mill, rolled into a corner of the yard and abandoned, while the rotten wooden post and stone trough still stand in the shadow of a new office-block. On the wooden roof of the shed at the back of the fire station is the faded legend:

· 'TEMPERANCE HALL'

Two fork-lift drivers sit in contented idleness, feet up on boxes, smoking and reading comics in the sunshine—no-one will be out to check on them for a few more minutes.

The new cars shine from the plate-glass windows of the sale room and only the railway walker knows about the heaps of mildewed tyres and rusting Austin bread vans that litter the oily wasteland by the disused line.

Public houses add spice to bland railway walks. When the fields each side are dull, the hedgerows devoid of interest, and the walk has become a succession of straights and curves unrolling under the boots, it is refreshing to body and spirit to pull off the track and find a friendly bar. Wet feet to the fire, glass in hand and map open, the walker's jaded appetite is renewed for the miles to come.

At Wiveliscombe I found a crowded, smoky public bar. Silence fell as I entered. The regular drinkers put down their pints, and took a lingering up-and-downer at my muddy boots and pockets bulging with maps, notes and camera. A few heads were shaken in disbelief, and more when I asked about buses—'On a Sunday? You must be joking. No chance!'

Everyone had resumed their drinks and conversation when the street door opened and a very senior citizen shuffled in, blinking behind thick spectacles. One of the domino players looked up aggressively as the old man peered at his hand.

'Who are you staring at, you four-eyed old git?'

The company turned to watch. I held my breath, waiting for an explosion of curses and fists. Suddenly the whole bar burst into laughter, including the domino player and the old man, who bent over his stick wheezing with delight. A joke strictly for local consumption.

Early morning is the time for spiders' webs. As the walker breasts the dense sunrise mist that heralds a hot day, the webs hang in sparkling chains from gorse bushes, piled one above another like arachnidan high-rise blocks. The first rays of the sun, breaking through onto the track, show up their amazing symmetry. In the dark dampness of deep cuttings, dawn can be suspended for hours. Long after the webs in the high bushes have dried to a mundane brown, those in the shadows retain their pearls. Birds wait for the spiders—and the cats wait for the birds.

In a thick early mist in the Exe Valley, I watched a tortoiseshell hunter crouching behind a tussock of grass by the concrete platform of Morebath Junction Halt. The tip of his tail twitched stiffly from side to side above the grass. He didn't see me, being intent on an unsuspecting thrush, which was hopping along the platform and pecking among the broken flakes of concrete.

Unseen by the tortoiseshell, but visible to me where I stood on the track, a ginger cat crept along the opposite hedge and settled into an identical position. I watched the cats, they stared at the thrush, and the thrush concentrated on his breakfast. This still-life remained frozen for a good five minutes, animated only by the twitching, tense tortoise-shell tail. Then by some subtle instinct the two cats seemed to become aware of each other's presence simultaneously. The ginger ears flattened. The tortoiseshell tail held still, poised at attention. The grass tussock rustled. With a chirrup of alarm, the thrush fluttered up and over the hedge. Ginger Ears turned tail and darted into the bushes. Tortoiseshell slipped across the track after him, and disappeared.

I let out my breath, and walked on. From somewhere behind me in the mist a terrible caterwauling broke out, screeching through the dawn hush, as Ginger Ears paid the price of untimely interference.

'My subjects were the grimy work-horses, in the twilight of their years, neglected, forlorn, but still working. In the gloomy depths of the great steam sheds, I found intense beauty of a most dramatic kind if I searched for it, through the dirt and grime. Shafts of sunlight penetrated through broken panes of soot-caked glass in the roof, through the

61

steam and smoke, and played on pools of green oil on the floor. Lovely harmonies could be found in the cool greys and browns and mauves of the engines; and, on the connecting rods, one could detect the occasional glint of brilliant light where wet, slowly dripping oil, caught the sun. The occasional wisp of steam would eddy up into the darkness of the roof and, although all seemed quiet, as the great steam engines were at rest ready to go out onto the road, there would always be a murmur of gentle sound as they simmered in the gloom.

'I am sure that if Rembrandt had been alive in the age of steam railways, he would have been a railway enthusiast. His sombre palette would have been ideal to record these "Cathedrals of Steam"—the scenes which have now passed into history.' Thus writes David Shepherd, wildlife artist and steam railway lover, in his *Guide to the East Somerset Railway, Cranmore.*

In their century and a half of dominance, steam engines collected a complete legend around their gaunt, appealing frames. Here was the trampling, fire-breathing iron horse of the prairies, the immense, distance-quelling Behemoth; also the lovable, almost cuddly branch line tank engine, puffing and fussing around its daily treadmill. In this one machine were caught the basic elements of fire, water, air and earth—strength and grace, character and simplicity.

When the smooth, silent diesel came from behind and overtook the mighty steam engine, all the ingredients of a classic confrontation were present. In one corner, the unfussy, efficient newcomer, streamlined to a standard pattern, quiet and clean—in the other corner the sweating, thrusting, red-hot old-timer, noisy, smelly, dirty, wasteful and compelling. But practically, economically, it was no contest. Steam died a king's death in the full glare of publicity, well-documented and much mourned.

Very occasionally one comes across a steam engine in the course of an old railway walk. A rusting, red-leaded freight locomotive waited in the cool of Radstock shed for restoration. This was BR No 53808, formerly Class 7F 2-8-0 No 88 of the Somerset & Dorset Joint Railway, saved from Barry scrapyard and the cutter's torch in 1970. The square, unpainted firebox tapered into the long rusty barrel of the boiler. On top, a circle of naked bolts awaited the crowning glory of the steam-dome. In the blank-eyed cab, dials and pipes had long been ripped out. Yet it smelt of hope, and of the optimism of its dedicated band of restorers.

At the opposite end of the country lies the NER branch line from the cobbled market town of Alston to grim Halt-whistle on the Carlisle—Newcastle main line. At Slaggyford Station between the slopes of the North Tyne valley, green and cream paint adorned the station buildings. On the other side of the single-track line, beyond the station house fence, a little green-painted saddle-tank engine stood beside the vegetable patch, lovingly restored by some patient hand.

Yet steam has no monopoly of sentimental attachment. The great wave of nostalgic sorrow generated by the phasing out a year or two ago of the Class 52 diesel-hydraulic loco-motives—the 'Westerns'—can hardly be explained away simply as regret for the passing of a group of efficient, reliable machines. It has much more to do with the fact that the 'Westerns' were all named, a much needed return to individuality which British Railways for some years tried to stamp out in the interest of rationalisation—fortunately a policy reversed by the recent limited return to naming. *Western Musketeer, Western Chieftain, Western Prince*—splendid, arrogant names which gave back that missing dignity and importance to the locomotive—*Western Ruler, Western Emperor, Western Nobleman, Western Monarch.*

On an April morning I halted by Stoke Canon level crossing, just where my chosen walking track curved away beside the river on its peaceful run north to Bampton. As I stood and admired the chocolate-and-cream GWR signalbox, a shirt-sleeved figure within moved over to the long row of levers and pulled one with a twang of wires. The rails began to hum. I waited, just on the off chance. I knew that most of the 'Westerns' had already been withdrawn from service; but perhaps, here in the heart of the Western Region . . .

A flat-faced locomotive flashed into view, shuttling past at speed with an eleven-coach express for Plymouth. On her blue flank, the silver name-plate left its message imprinted in the memory long after the train had vanished round the curve—*Western Empress.*

PART II

Some railway walks

8 THE SOMERSET & DORSET— BATH TO BOURNEMOUTH

Day 1

Bath Green Park station at 10.45 am on a hot August day. I stood in gleaming new boots in front of the station building, reading the peeling posters stuck over the doors of the booking hall.

The building—of listed architectural importance, but allowed to fall into decay since the Somerset & Dorset line was closed in 1966—looked hollow and broken. The columns of the neo-Georgian frontage framed smashed windows and climbing weeds, and the arched glass roof over the cast-iron train shed had been shattered by time and vandals' stones. Cars were parked in rows between the platforms where the trains used to stand.

From railway station to car park was a natural transition, as the owners and would-be owners, British Railways and Bath Corporation, had been locked in indecisive negotiations for eight years. Various schemes for the building were mooted during the intervening years; in the archives of the *Bath Chronicle* are suggestions for swimming pools, recreation centres, sports arenas, theatres, museums and community centres. Bath Corporation did at last clinch the purchase. But the building still crumbles, unused, waiting for the by now inevitable demolition order to complete the sad story of neglect.

I turned my back on the brown paint and rusty cream ironwork of the station, and set out on the first of the 71½ miles to Bournemouth. At Bath Junction, where the S & D trains used to leave Midland Railway metals and swing away south-east through a 180° curve on to their own single-track line, the connecting viaduct had disappeared. I scrambled over banks and building sites to rejoin the line on a short stretch of linear park. This is a scheme by Bath Corporation to provide a strip of green land along the old railway where the children from nearby housing estates can play safely. Locomotives needed a good head of steam here, to carry them up the 1 in 50 incline out of Bath.

The linear park ended at the mouth of the Devonshire tunnel, now earthed and grassed over. On the far side, the Lyncombe Vale nature trail runs in a deep cutting up to the entrance of the second tunnel on the incline—the notorious Combe Down tunnel. This was the longest unventilated tunnel in Britain, running for over a mile under the southern outskirts of Bath and emerging into open countryside. It was the building of Combe Down tunnel in 1874 that broke the original Somerset & Dorset Railway Company, forcing it to sell out to the Midland and the London & South Western railways, which ran the line jointly until the 1923 Grouping. The engine crews had a very rough ride here, with smoke and sulphurous fumes beating down round them from the low tunnel roof. Northbound crews got the worst of it, with their locomotives going at little more than walking speed as they laboured up from Midford.

I gave myself an easier task, detouring by side streets over the top of the tunnel to Tucking Mill viaduct, set like a giant in the woods of Horsecombe Vale. The track led south through cornfields and the green bowls of wooded Avon countryside.

Midford Station on its steep hillside was marked by just one overgrown platform. All the buildings had disappeared, and the eight-arched Midford viaduct beyond was impenetrably wired up. The viaduct once carried the Somerset & Dorset over four separate obstacles—the Bath to Frome road, the Cam brook, the Somersetshire Coal Canal, and the Great Western branch line from Hallatrow via Camerton (where that tortured nineteenth century diarist the Reverend John Skinner suffered such indignities at the hands of the uncouth miners who were his parishioners) to Limpley Stoke. This was the Cam Valley branch, which found fame as the setting for two film comedies, *The Titfield Thunderbolt* and *The Ghost Train*. On the far side of the viaduct, the double-track line commenced.

Wellow station, two miles down the line, was patronised as much as any on the Somerset & Dorset, serving a village

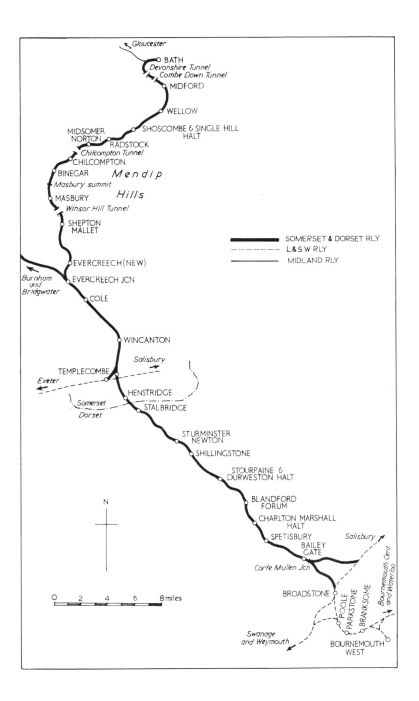

Gloucester

BATH
Devonshire Tunnel
Combe Down Tunnel
MIDFORD

WELLOW

SHOSCOMBE & SINGLE HILL
HALT

MIDSOMER
NORTON
RADSTOCK
Chilcompton Tunnel
CHILCOMPTON

BINEGAR   *Mendip*
Masbury summit
MASBURY   *Hills*
Winsor Hill Tunnel

SHEPTON
MALLET

SOMERSET & DORSET RLY
L & S W RLY
MIDLAND RLY

EVERCREECH(NEW)

Burnham
and
Bridgwater

EVERCREECH JCN

COLE

WINCANTON

Salisbury

TEMPLECOMBE

Exeter

HENSTRIDGE
Somerset   STALBRIDGE
Dorset

STURMINSTER
NEWTON

SHILLINGSTONE

STOURPAINE &
DURWESTON HALT

BLANDFORD
FORUM

CHARLTON MARSHALL
HALT

SPETISBURY   Salisbury
BAILEY
GATE

Corfe Mullen Jcn

N

BROADSTONE

POOLE
PARKSTONE
BRANKSOME

Bournemouth Cent.
and Waterloo

Swanage
and Weymouth

BOURNEMOUTH
WEST

0   2   4   6   8 miles

which lies at the bottom of deep valleys in all directions. This was an example of the advantage that country railways enjoyed over buses, which nowadays struggle infrequently up and down the steep roads to the village. Wellow station has found a new lease of life as a private home, restored and neat. S&D stations were strongly and simply built, and a number have been saved from deterioration by private owners.

I walked on in the hot afternoon sunshine, past Shoscombe and Single Hill Halt, which the villagers had to wait for until 1929; they only got it then because the LMS was locked in battle with the motor bus. The track now runs into the fringe of the North Somerset coal-mining district. The Somerset & Dorset provided a valuable outlet for the coal to reach the industrial Midlands, and many of the collieries had a short spur connecting them to the S&D main line. On the left were the abandoned stone buildings and pithead gear of Writhlington Colliery. A child's screams and a dog's barking echoed among the silent buildings. It was hard to imagine the blood-stained night of 7 August, 1876, when this peaceful spot was the scene of the worst accident in the history of the Somerset & Dorset. In those days the section between Radstock and Wellow was single-track; here, on that bank holiday night just over a century ago, a confused and over-worked 16-year-old signalman gave the order which caused two trains to meet in head-on collision near Foxcote signal-box. Twelve passengers and one of the guards were killed.

From Writhlington, sleepers led into Radstock, where the big grey stone engine shed and small station building still stand. Radstock remembers its tough coal-mining past. Reminders are all around in the shape of slag-heaps on the Mendip slopes. The town has always had a reputation as a hard place—Victorian ladies, advertising in the *Bath Chronicle* for domestic servants, often added a rider: 'No Radstock girl need apply'.

Day 2

There are two disused level crossings in the middle of Radstock in the bottom of the valley. The North crossing carried the Somerset & Dorset over the Bath—Shepton Mallet road towards the Mendips. A few yards further south was the crossing from Radstock West station, which took the Great Western Railway out in the direction of Bristol—the Bristol & North Somerset line. On a bank holiday Saturday, road and rail traffic reached such a peak here that frustrated drivers, pinched between the two level crossings, wished they had never heard of the motor car—or the steam engine!

Early next morning I climbed over the locked S&D crossing gates, and set off to climb the Mendips. The track mounted steadily at 1 in 50, crossing the zig-zag Five Arches viaduct over the grassy track of the GWR line, and passed slag heaps and colliery sidings.

Midsomer Norton station, two miles above Radstock, used to win the 'best kept station' award year after year with its beautiful flower displays. Ten years after closure, there were only wild roses growing pergola-style up the rusty lattice-work LSWR signal at the end of the platform. The station buildings, shuttered and boarded, are not as useless as they look, Somerset Education Committee having had the vision to convert them to a field study centre for local schools.

Beyond the station, the long, stiff climb of the Mendips begins in earnest. The twenty-six miles from Bath to Evercreech Junction did not form part of the original Somerset & Dorset. That unassuming railway, born in 1862 of a marriage between the Somerset Central and Dorset Central Railways, ran from Burnham-on-Sea to Wimborne, and later to Bournemouth. The Bath extension from Evercreech was added in 1874, in a bid to attract traffic from the Midlands to the South Coast by a direct cross-country route.

When the Somerset & Dorset Joint Railway Company built the extension, the Mendip Hills presented them with a formidable obstacle. Money was tight, as always, which made extensive tunnelling operations impossible; the railway thus had to climb the limestone barrier in long twisting sections to its culmination at Masbury Summit, 811ft above sea level, before dropping down the long slopes into Bath. Southbound trains, leaving Radstock, had to climb at an almost unbroken 1 in 50 for 7½ miles, before they could plunge thankfully down the other side of the Mendips

In the Radstock area not only was the Somerset & Dorset line closed but also the former Great Western branch from Frome to Bristol, which passed under the Somerset & Dorset at Five Arches Bridge. *Above:* A Somerset & Dorset line goods train leaves Radstock and crosses the Great Western line. *(Ivo Peters).* *Below:* The bridge still stands but the tracks have gone. *(C J F Somerville)*

towards Dorset. For the walker, swinging along on an even surface, 1 in 50 may not seem a very arduous climb, but the steam engines, their wheels straining for a grip on the rails, often hauling more than 350 tons, found the slope a tough challenge, especially when mist or drizzle (not unknown over the Mendips) made contact between steel wheels and rails slippery.

Double-heading—two engines in harness—or banking, where one engine pulls and another pushes from the rear, was necessary for most trains on their passage over the summit, though the sturdy 7F 2-8-0s, specially designed for the problems posed by the Somerset & Dorset, were allowed to take ten coaches unassisted. In 1960 a new type of loco-motive was introduced successfully to the S&D—the BR Class 9F 2-10-0, which pulled loads up to 410 tons with no assistance. But as the line had only six more years of life ahead of it when they came on the scene, their full potential was never realised. 'Evening Star', the last steam engine to be built by BR, was one of the 9Fs set to work on the S&D.

The track climbs ever upwards, past the twin mouths of the Chilcompton tunnel, through cuttings with ferns clinging to the rocky limestone walls. I passed gaunt old quarry build-ings housing a decaying collection of machinery—massive iron hoists and furnaces, mildewed leather belts and bellows. On each side were the enormous scooped-out semi-circles of the quarries. Past Binegar station, whimsically renamed 'Boiland' by some salad-loving producer in a 1956 BR instruc-tional film. Up and up, towards the humped iron age fort of Masbury Ring and the summit of the climb over the Mendips.

At last the track levelled out. Masbury station, just beyond the summit, occupies a bleak and lonely spot on the Mendip ridge. Unlike the other stations on the Bath extension, it had no toothed wooden awning over the platform to protect its passengers from wind and weather. The station master's house on the platform boasts a stone carving above its bay window. It depicts a medieval castle with the legend 'Maes-bury Castle'—a name borrowed from the Iron Age fort which looms over the summit.

Glastonbury Tor and the Vale of Avalon were hazy in the heat below as I crunched on ballast over Ham Woods via-duct. Ahead were the twin bores of Winsor Hill tunnel, the right-hand one clear, the left blocked by a steel barrier, bearing a notice warning trespassers of radioactive waste material within—a sinister note in the quiet hills. Ivo Peters' marvellous photographic record *The Somerset & Dorset— An English Cross-Country Railway* recounts an incident during the harsh winter of 1962/3, when a goods train was buried in snow drifts up here for three days.

Beyond the tunnel the track led between young conifers into Shepton Mallet. Here one of the major engineering features of the S&D is still to be seen—the twenty-seven arches of Charlton viaduct, which carried the track high above the valley into the station at Charlton Road.

Up to Cannards Grave I trudged, where Mr Cannard paid the ultimate penalty for sheep stealing a couple of centuries before. A hanging human silhouette with a border of sheep is depicted on an inn sign at the crossroads on the A37 where the thief's remains are supposed to be buried. I walked on by fields where the cuttings have been filled in by farmers, and at nightfall into the little village of Evercreech.

Day 3

Overnight the weather did a swift about-turn, and a rainy wind battered me as I stood next morning on the site of Evercreech New Station, on a track carpeted with garden-escaped primulas. Away to the right, the Somerset & Dorset branch line curved away on its flat run across the Vale of Avalon and the peat moors to Burnham-on-Sea. The Bath extension enabled the Company to build Evercreech New on the edge of the village itself. Before then, the inhabitants had to make do with a station two miles from Evercreech—a station which became a busy place when the Mendip route was opened up. This was Evercreech Junction, where the engines were based which helped to bring heavy expresses and goods trains up the steep bank to Masbury Summit, and where the Burnham line began its journey. The porters at the Junction had a distinctive cry for arriving trains— 'Evercreeeeeeeeeech . . . Junc—SHERN!' By the level crossing, the former Railway Hotel has been poignantly renamed *The Silent Whistle*.

Long straight stretches of track led me southwards through dripping woods and fields. The red brick station master's house behind Cole Station overlooks the grey limestone building on the platform, the furthest example to the north of Dorset Central Railway design with high gables and chimneys. Just north of here was the point where the Dorset Central and Somerset Central linked up to form the joint railway.

72

Above: The former Somerset & Dorset line Glastonbury & Street station on the branch from Evercreech to Burnham on Sea is now a timber yard. *(C J F Somerville). Below:* Midsomer Norton station on the former Somerset & Dorset line, despite removal of the tracks, still has a semaphore signal in position which serves to support climbing rose bushes. *(C J F Somerville)*

Gently rolling land lay to each side with woods, fields, scattered houses, and a church nestling under a brow of hills. The track stretched away dead straight as far as the eye could see, in contrast to the contortions of the Mendip section.

Wincanton was loud with lorries; a vast pack crouched at ease outside the St Ivel depot. From here the S&D ran due south for four miles into the pretty little village of Templecombe, where it met and passed under the main LSWR line from Exeter to Waterloo. Many junctions and spurs of track crossed and interchanged there, and Templecombe was once a busy railway centre; since 1966 most bed and breakfast places there have shut up shop. I settled for the pub at nearby Horsington.

Day 4

With the help of Ivo Peters' photographs, next morning in Templecombe I worked out the route among the grassy tracks of disused spurs diverging to different junctions and sidings, and started on the sixteen miles to Blandford Forum.

The countryside was flatter now, with wooded hills in the distance. Henstridge Station was full of rusty cars and barbed wire. Grasshoppers chirruped in the dry grass on the track, which ran straight ahead through Stalbridge, blue and misty in the heat.

Over the Dorset border, the market town of Sturminster Newton lies on the banks of the peaceful River Stour. Several centuries of building styles stand against each other in the main street. The road drops down to a medieval bridge over the Stour, which bears a plaque warning would-be vandals of their liability to transportation. It is a lovely green spot, with anglers fishing the mill pond, water lilies, and a riverside pub selling mild ale and bread and cheese. I ate and drank in the shade of trees, then shouldered my pack and moved back to the railway by the busy market place.

The track ran past beautiful old Fiddleford Mill, set behind pollarded willows beside the wide bends of the Stour. The afternoon sun blazed down on water meadows. A fox bounded in great leaps over a cornfield into the shade of the hedge.

Shillingstone station was slightly grander than the average Dorset Central station. It boasted a platform canopy, provided to keep the rain off King Edward VII, who used the station when visiting Iwerne Minster House, nearby. Beyond the station lay the last five miles, broken by a road detour to avoid a dismantled bridge over the river, twenty yards wide at this point. The ploughed soil on each side of the track showed white chalk beneath. Bright yellow mustard plants shone in the evening sunlight.

Blandford Forum is an old market town with an important place in Dorset history. It has several times been in the centre of battles, but the medieval buildings in the town managed to survive until the Georgians carried out a comprehensive reconstruction. Nowadays modern housing estates line the outskirts, but towards the centre the streets run sharply up and down, with Georgian civic buildings dominating the scene.

I descended the narrow streets to my hotel, very glad to rest my blistered feet.

Day 5

I rejoined the Somerset & Dorset in a long, cool cutting on the fringe of Blandford. The track was laid out for a double line of railway here, in pleasant contrast to the sixteen narrow single-track miles between Templecombe and Blandford; a broad path, easy on the feet.

Two miles on is Charlton Marshall Halt, another station built in response, not to the pleas of local residents, but to competition from the internal combustion engine. It was opened in 1928, nearly seventy years after the railway arrived in the district, and it was closed ten years before the rest of the S&D. With such a short life-span, and serving a tiny community, the Halt was never a very grand affair. Now its platforms were almost hidden under thorn bushes and brambles. The nameboards were still there, giving the place a special atmosphere of desolation—a name, but no life. Sunlight filtered through layers of leaves overhead before striking the platforms and track with a green, gloomy light.

The line hereabouts runs through some of the most attractive and unspoilt countryside along the whole route. Past Sturminster Marshall, the first traces of sand were visible in the soil, together with those characteristic coastal plants, gorse and heather and a preponderance of conifers.

At Corfe Mullen Junction, the track narrowed to become single-track again, and the old Dorset Central line to

Wimborne branched off to the east, overgrown and impenetrable, closed since 1933. Ahead lay three miles of sand cuttings, pine trees and a golf course, before the drop of 1 in 97 into Broadstone station. As Somerset & Dorset trains ran from Broadstone into Bournemouth on track belonging to the London & South Western Railway, these were the last three miles of S&D territory. I pushed between patches of gorse and birch suckers. The vegetation was arid—that combination of dry, sandy soil and dark, prickly bushes that heralds the sea. The track ran between heather-covered sandy cliffs. Everywhere yellow, purple and ochre met the eye. High above the line grew the famous pine trees that lent their name to the Somerset & Dorset's renowned 'Pines Express'.

The other side of the golf course was Broadstone Junction station, cut off from the overgrown S&D track by a stout wire fence, its dilapidated buildings facing the boundary of the Somerset & Dorset.

Day 6

The final eight miles of the route lie in the heart of Bournemouth, one of the most built-up and heavily populated coastal resorts in England. This was the prize at the end of the line, for company, customers and train crews alike.

I walked down the rusty rails from Broadstone to Poole station, where I caught a train to Branksome—the only part of the whole trip on which one can actually follow the path of Somerset & Dorset trains by rail.

From Branksome station a long road of hotels led towards the site of Bournemouth West station, now a sandy, banked-up building site, bisected by a newly constructed road, and a car park surrounded by tall hotels.

The only visible remnants of the Somerset & Dorset Railway's seaside terminus are two green railway lamps protruding from the car park wall, still in position where they were first placed to light the evening passengers from the trains.

9 LYME REGIS TO AXMINSTER

The little Dorsetshire resort of Lyme Regis, after being without railway accommodation to the present time, is now to be connected with the system of 'iron roads' that has spread over the length and breadth of our land. The Axminster and Lyme Regis Light Railway, is now completed, and will be opened for traffic as soon as the earth works are sufficiently consolidated . . ."

(*The Railway Magazine*, Vol 13, 1903)

The low station building squatted on its crumbling platform, the slatted wooden walls peeling and flaking with years of neglect. The crenellations of the valances, once trim in green and cream paint, resembled broken, dirty teeth, throwing the shuttered and boarded windows into deep shadow.

The Axminster & Lyme Regis Light Railway was opened for passenger and goods traffic on 24 August, 1903; when I stood on the grass-grown platform at Lyme Regis, ten years had passed since the last engine groaned its way up the bank towards Uplyme and the hills.

A blackbird sang and hopped under the blank concrete station nameboards as I set off on the seven mile walk to Axminster. Foxgloves and bushes of buddleia sprouted along the track, concealing a deep cavity beside the path—an engine inspection pit, over which the locomotives which worked this rural branch line once hissed as their ashpans were raked out. Towards the end of the line's lifespan, three Adams 4-4-2 tank engines handled all the traffic that passed between Axminster and Lyme Regis. From 1959 most of the work was done by No 30583, rejuvenated by a general overhaul. It was a well-loved personality to those who used the

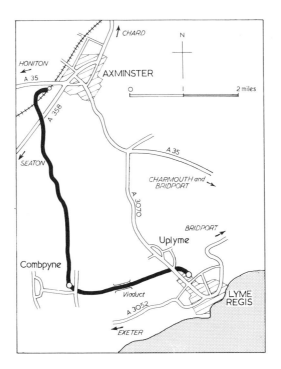

line. The little Adams tanks fulfilled the two main require-
ments of the Lyme Regis branch—not too heavy for the
shaky Cannington viaduct, and powerful enough to master
gradients of up to 1 in 40.

The track wound upwards towards Uplyme, perched high
above Lyme Bay. Contractors, with a practical eye on cost
and effort saving, had used the materials nearest to hand in
building the line. Bridges were neatly constructed of flat
nuggets of flint, extracted from the cuttings as they were
driven through the hills around Lyme Regis. Climbing into
higher country, the view opened out. Picked out in dark
green and yellow, hillocks and wooded slopes fell away to
the sea.

A fine piece of railway architecture appeared ahead—the
nine graceful arches of the Cannington viaduct, spanning a
deep valley and dominating the huddle of farm roofs below.
The contemporary *Railway Magazine* description includes
some interesting constructional details, and gives a good
example of cost-cutting ingenuity in the use of local materials:

78

The Cannington Valley viaduct is the great feature of the new railway from an engineering point of view; in fact, it may be said to have rendered the whole undertaking practicable by making unnecessary the tunnel involved in most previous schemes . . . the modern practice of using mass concrete in bridge-building has very greatly reduced the cost of such structures; and, in the case of the viaduct in question, crushed flints from the adjacent cutting yielded a suitable material for the manufacture of the concrete without the admixture of sand . . . The fears of the engineer as to the suitability of the soil of the hills for tunnelling have been confirmed by his experience in one of the cuttings near Lyme Regis, where the treacherous green-sand has slipped persistently, necessitating the sides of the cutting being supported by a timber breastwork with a backing of corrugated iron sheets.

These treacherous shifting sands were the bane of the navvies' lives. In fact, the shifting sands in the valley floor later forced the company to add a strengthening pier under the third arch from the Axminster end of the viaduct, and they proved a constant threat to the viaduct's safety throughout the life of the line. From the middle of the slim structure a magnificent panorama greeted holidaymakers bound for Lyme Regis, with the stratified brows of the cliffs where Mary Anning once dug for ammonites, marching away on the fringe of the sea.

The deep cutting beyond, whence came the crushed flints for the viaduct, was lined with more dense clumps of fox-gloves. Baby thrushes swerved drunkenly about in the first throes of learning to fly, while anxious parents scurried and flapped in the brambles. The track led on between thickets of fir trees to the station at Combpyne, a small hamlet for which the 1903 *Railway Magazine* envisaged a splendid future, catering for those twin British virtues, snobbery and hypochondria:

At present there is scarcely any population hereabouts except at Rousden, the beautiful cliff estate of Sir Wilfrid Peek; but there is excellent scope for the development of accommodation for visitors, the site being an ideal one for the erection of a hydropathic establishment or residential hotel.

A wire barrier sealed off the section of line past the station buildings, which are still in use. At the top of the station cutting, a hoop of rusty metal was buried in the chalky soil— part of an ancient gin-trap, its semi-circles of sharp teeth set on sprung jaws, attached to a stout iron peg to hold it firmly in the earth.

Beyond the station the track ran into the overgrown Combpyne Woods. The trees came right down to the edge of the line, their massed ranks broken here and there by banks of bracken. Some of the bracken fronds were still not fully open. So dense was the shade cast by the overhanging trees that they would never get the sunlight they needed to come to full maturity.

Below the level of the old railway track, deep ravines criss-crossed the woods. Giant beech trees lay in the depths where they had fallen, ferns and fungi growing on the rotten trunks. The trackbed was thickly covered with last year's fallen leaves, and a profound silence reigned.

The open fields around Axminster appeared ahead between the trees, and soon the track left the shady woods and ran along in farmland between low hills. The scatter of houses that marked the town came closer. In the derelict shell of a platelayer's hut, a mass of hen feathers littered the floor. Cold ashes were piled in one corner, showing where an unscrupulous wayfarer had cooked the meal he had probably poached from the nearby farm.

A low embankment carried the track beside the flat water-meadows of the River Axe. It crossed a bridge over the Exeter to Waterloo line, and trailed round to run down a short, steep incline parallel to the main line. The green path completed its seven mile journey from the sea at an over-grown platform in Axminster Station.

The passenger service was always influenced by the seasonal nature of the traffic, but, summer or winter, trains for Lyme Regis never departed from Axminster until their main-line connections had arrived, however delayed these might be. Patience was a necessary virtue in a traveller on the Lyme Regis railway; but once under way he could sit back and enjoy the timeless charm of the backwoods branch line to the sea.

Much of the former Axminster and Lyme Regis branch is still traceable, partly because after the withdrawal of BR services and closure of the line a narrow gauge railway scheme was planned to be laid over part of the route but did not in fact materialise as envisaged. Here, almost at the end of its life, a train leaves Axminster for Lyme Regis in February 1965. *(John Goss)*

10 THE SHOREHAM TO CHRIST'S HOSPITAL BRIDLEWAY

At the foot of the South Downs is the tiny, ancient Sussex church of St Botolph's, built of flint. It stands as an isolated remnant of the flourishing community recorded here on the banks of the River Adur in the Domesday Book.

Between the church and the river runs the green track of the former London Brighton & South Coast Railway branch from Shoreham-on-Sea, two miles down river, through the gap carved in the Downs by the Adur, to Christ's Hospital. Within two years of its closure, in 1966, West Sussex County Council had bought up the old railway track, and it now forms a bridleway and footpath through the heart of rural Sussex.

St Botolph's Church makes an interesting starting-point for the sixteen-mile walk. The track runs north beside the river, across the route of the South Downs Way long-distance footpath, and past the site of Bramber station where the lineside buildings and trees are smothered under thick green mats of clematis. The re-surfaced trackbed makes for easy walking, and there are views to the west and east of the steep ramparts of the Downs.

Just beyond the little market town of Steyning, a mile up the line from Bramber, a deep cutting has been filled in with a mountainous rubbish dump, a villainous heap picked over by crows and black-backed gulls. The intrepid walker who climbs to the top of the cutting is rewarded with a superb aspect of the old railway stretching away across the flat river plain of the Adur, crossing the river on reconstructed concrete bridges. In autumn, the red and brown of the bushes along the tracksides contrast handsomely with the wide

82

Although one line survives on the Isle of Wight, from Ryde to Shanklin, now worked by electric trains, the original route continued on from Shanklin through Wroxall to Ventnor, from which the track has now been removed. This section, though, includes a long tunnel under the chalk downs on the south side of the island. *Above:* In 1965, a year before closure, a train is seen about to leave Wroxall for Ventnor. *(John Goss).* *Below:* Parts of the former branch line from Guildford to Horsham and from Horsham to Shoreham by Sea have been converted into a bridleway while some sections have been taken for road schemes. A train from Guildford to Horsham is seen here approaching Bramley & Wonersh in May 1965. *(John Goss)*

green meadows on each side. Here the Adur has sliced the solid wall of the South Downs in two; to the west is Chanctonbury Ring, to the east the foot of Devil's Dyke.

In creating the bridleway, the County Council experimented with applications of top soil and grass seed; but the yielding surface was cut up badly by the horses' hooves, and in the main the path has been left as a beaten earth track, with most of the maintenance effort concentrated on drainage, a special problem in a river valley. Well signposted, the track leads on to Henfield, where a new housing estate has been built over the station site, with an appropriate name—'The Beechings'!

Two miles further on, at Partridge Green, a new factory complex sprawls across the station yard, dominating the tumbledown railway buildings beyond. Other industrial and residential developments are planned on the old railway track, which makes one appreciate even more the foresight of the West Sussex County Council in planning the bridleway so soon after the closure of the line, and before the new constructions could spoil the continuity of the path. A touring camp site with a camping area, picnic place, restaurant and petrol station is planned for the station site at West Grinstead, where the line runs below a bridge in a high-sided, overgrown cutting. The LBSCR brought the railway to the inhabitants of this small village—but they had to walk a good mile to get to their station.

Shaggy 'ink-caps' or Coprinus fungi grow in quantities on the track in this part, and the lineside woods make coverts for both common and golden pheasant. At Copsale an old signal stands proudly in a cottage garden. The bridleway signposts also carry arms marking the crossing places of footpaths, but in most cases they seem to have been absorbed without trace in the adjoining cornfields.

Approaching Southwater, two miles from the junction with the main Horsham line at Christ's Hospital, the tall chimneys of Horsham brickworks make an abrupt contrast to the hitherto rural scene. Enormous bowls of clay have been scooped out of the ground, with corrugated-iron tunnels snaking up and down the earthworks, sheltering miles of conveyor belt. Piles of good, indifferent and bad bricks of all shapes, sizes and colours are heaped up, with the misshapen

84

rejects tumbled higgledy-piggledy into the ditches beside the line. Southwater station building, a neat unit comprising a two-storey house and single-storey offices and waiting room, still stands on its platform, with brambles making inexorable progress up the walls. The whole site is earmarked for the development of shops, parking, a new church and other facilities, as part of the long-term Southwater village plan.

The path skirts round a succession of fenced gardens across the track, and emerges for a final mile of level walking to the junction. To the right is the spacious parkland of Christ's Hospital school, surrounded by well-grown trees. The school removed to Sussex from London in 1902, and the LBSCR, hoping for an accompanying boom in housing development, opened a handsome station on the main line just north of the school. The development never took place, and the station cannot be seen from the junction—technically named Itchingfield Junction after the nearby hamlet. The bridleway ends at a post-and-wire fence which marks off the path from the electrified main line.

By detouring round the school, the walker can join the northern section of the West Sussex County Council's bridleway, which runs from Christ's Hospital station through the Slinfold nature reserve (see Appendix A, No 101) to Baynards tunnel. At Baynards, he can continue along the Baynards to Bramley railway path established by Surrey County Council (see Appendix A, No 87).

11 THE MID-WALES RAILWAY—BUILTH WELLS TO NEWBRIDGE-ON-WYE

The railway map of Wales nowadays resembles a spider's web with the heart neatly cut out. The coastal lines have largely survived, thanks to their steady volume of holiday traffic and the demands of the industrial ports. The West Coast lines thread together the holiday resorts, and from Cardiff thin fingers of track stick up into the South Wales mining valleys.

But a glance at the Welsh heartland—the hills and mountains, populated by small farming communities and market towns—tells a sadly familiar story of lines built in high hopes, which spent most of their lives struggling against sparse traffic and high running costs, and which eventually fell victim to post-war depression and the Beeching axe.

A grassy path runs from the small town of Builth Wells north-westwards to Newbridge-on-Wye, hugging the right bank of the wide, slow-moving River Wye as it flows south on its winding course to Chepstow. Some of the loneliest and most beautiful scenery in Britain can be seen from the track: immense, rolling hills, their sides covered with bracken and their tops thinly clad with rough grass, and, in contrast, deeper in the valley of the Wye, fields whose hedges run in dark lines outwards from the river to the feet of the hills. Buzzards plane above dense woodland, and herons fish from the islets in mid-river.

These peaceful, isolated five miles of green lane form part of the fifty-five-mile corridor through the heart of Wales which is all that is left today of the Mid-Wales Railway, a line that held a special place in the affections of railway enthusiasts and country lovers for almost a century. Built like so many Welsh railways with ambitions to become a lucrative through-route between England and the Welsh coast, the MWR was opened to passengers on 21 September 1864, from Tal-y-Llyn, four miles east of Brecon, to Moat Lane junction in the north. At the junction passengers could turn west to Aberystwyth and Pwllheli, or east to Oswestry and Wrexham.

Builth Wells station has remained empty since the closure of the Mid-Wales line on 30 December 1962. It stands on an island in a sea of weeds—rosebay willowherb, sorrel, thistles and nettles—station house and offices joined together in a long building of orange and grey stone, whose interior is darkened by ancient Great Western Railway brown paint. The other side of a new roundabout, the ballast scar of the track shows up as it curves away towards the tree-lined River Wye, upstream from the arched bridge leading to the town. The peace of the riverside scene is broken only by the clatter and hum of a huge quarry that disfigures the hillside above the station.

As I strolled along on a warm August afternoon, smooth grass gave way beneath my boots to rough ballast, with field bindweed and toadflax in the verges. The railway was built on a shelf running above the river and below the road, but fifteen years have crumbled away the track formation, and the line has to be followed from the road, looking down on the ramrod straight columns of great mulleins growing on the loose scree above the river. On the track again, I walked beside the Wye, now rushing over shallow rapids, with curving hills away to the north and west. Heavy resinous smells of burning pine-wood came from the forestry plantations.

At Builth Road, the MWR passed under the Central Wales Extension Railway from Knighton to Llandovery. The MWR station was Builth Road (Low Level); a fine, two-storey house which is now a pub, with a railway-minded landlord and a faded GWR poster map on the bar wall, advertising the Cambrian Coast to holidaymakers. Looming over the pub is the large, ugly CWER station building—Builth Road (High Level)—in puce brick.

The track leads past a timber yard under the bridge, and turns into a well-made farm track between thick hedges. Caerwnon House stands impressively among trees above the line, twin gables and tall chimneys in sturdy red brick. Gorse lines the sides of the shallow cuttings, and the track climbs into shady woodland of oak, silver birch and larch. Brushing through overhanging branches, I disturbed a tawny owl which lumbered heavily away over the trees, pursued by greenfinches. This is deep, wild country, where the eye is constantly drawn towards the distant hills. The track mounts a long bank through the woods, hacked out of the cliff on a high ledge above the Wye.

The River Ithon, a tributary as wide as the Wye itself, flows down to join the parent river beneath a tall viaduct of four piers, pierced with hollow arches. True to form, the dismantlers had made away with the decking, and I scrambled down precariously through the trees to ford the river, ankle-deep in clear water over slippery stones. Round-topped rusty boundary markers stuck out of the sheer sides of the railway embankment, showing the forgotten frontiers of the GWR, which took over the line in 1922. Gorse seed-pods snapped and crackled like Rice Krispies as they burst in the heat of the sun.

Near Newbridge, the track runs beside a low-lying area of marsh, studded with clumps of alder, willow and rushes, known as 'The Bog'. The spire of All Saints' Church at Newbridge-on-Wye appeared ahead, backed by Dôl-y-fan hill. A GWR signal post, its quadrant arm buried in the ground, lay full-length beside the path. The small station yard has vanished, and from the station bridge I looked down on neat new houses and gardens built across the track. To the north, the Mid-Wales Railway curved away towards Rhayader, with the Wye for company.

12 THE POTTERIES LOOPLINE GREENWAY—GOLDENHILL TO COBRIDGE

The main spine of the Stoke-on-Trent Greenway system of footpaths along old railways runs from Goldenhill in the north to Cobridge in the south. Based on the old Potteries Loop Line, closed in March 1964, it links the three most northerly of the Six Towns, Tunstall, Burslem and Hanley.

In 1968, the City of Stoke-on-Trent possessed more derelict land than any other local authority in the country, thanks to the enormous number of worked-out marl holes and colliery tips, and their lines of railway. There was only one acre of public open space for every 500 people. Drastic action was needed in a city which increasing numbers of people were leaving to find a more pleasant environment in which to live. The city council inaugurated a comprehensive programme of land reclamation, the largest of its kind ever undertaken, to bring the derelict land back under control, and the disused railways were included in the plan. To quote from the council's programme for derelict land reclamation:

> Although they will provide valuable local access to the major reclamation projects, the outstanding social significance of the Greenways is that they will make communication between different parts of the City an attractive recreational activity.

The level of grant aid set by the Local Government Act of 1966 was 50 per cent, but after strong representations by the council, a 75 per cent grant was fixed for Stoke-on-Trent.

The main Greenway starts on the northern outskirts of Tunstall, facing down a wide valley towards the massed roofs and chimneys of the city. On each side of the embankment on which the path runs, the ground rises in jagged terraces of

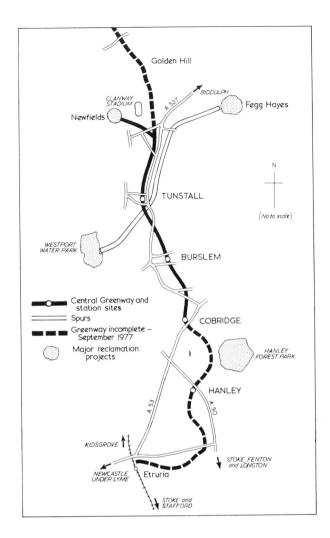

Golden Hill

CLANWAY
STADIUM

BIDDULPH

Fegg Hayes

Newfields

A.527

N

(No to scale)

TUNSTALL

WESTPORT
WATER PARK

BURSLEM

Central Greenway and
station sites

Spurs

Greenway incomplete –
September 1977

Major reclamation
projects

COBRIDGE

HANLEY
FOREST PARK

HANLEY

A 53

A 50

KIDSGROVE

STOKE, FENTON
and LONGTON

NEWCASTLE
UNDER LYME

Etruria

STOKE and
STAFFORD

worked-out delvings. Gorse and broom flourish, interspersed
with clumps of ragwort. Bright new houses are going up all
round on waste land, backed by the sombre purple brick of
the older terraced housing and large, heavy civic buildings,
churches and chapels.

Footpaths thread the coarse vegetation of the derelict land
each side to join the Greenway. Pools and ponds have been
created below the embankment, and among the planted birch
and maples are benches made of old railway sleepers. After

an initial mile on greasy grey clay, the walker treads an even surface of red shale, brought from burned-out coal tips.

Just before the site of Tunstall station, the path passes two 5ft locomotive wheels on a plinth, whose plaque commemorates the opening of the Tunstall section of the Greenway on 19 April 1972. To the right is Clanway sports stadium, constructed inside a disused marl hole, utilising its natural amphitheatre shape. The general atmosphere of the route is of excellent intentions well carried out, but spoiled in many places by vandalism with young trees and shrubs slashed, and aerosol graffiti sprayed over information boards. The instructive posters are attractively designed and hand drawn, laying out in detail the whole Greenway system and all the adjacent reclamation schemes.

The station bridge at Tunstall is lined with corrugated plastic, and the echoing path emerges by an old signal on to the station site—a quiet green channel between ugly black factory walls. In faded capitals on the wall of the Glazed and Floor Tile Clearing House the legend 'LONDON AND NORTH WESTERN RAILWAY CO. GOODS DEPOT' can be deciphered. The circular windows are fitted with cast-iron grilles, worked with a stylised design of locomotive wheels. The vandals have had fun with notices in the station road—'Authorised Barking Only'—'No Barking in front of Main Entrance'.

Beyond the station, a spur runs from the Greenway to another major reclamation scheme—the Westport Water Park. The Scotia Road viaduct which linked Tunstall to Burslem has been demolished, but on the Burslem side is a treat for Great Western fans far from home: the empty-tubed smokebox and chimney of GWR 2-8-0 freight locomotive, No 3817, positioned on the spot where Richard Marsh, then Chairman of British Rail, opened the Burslem section on 30 April 1973. Port Vale Football Club's stadium rears its patched and shabby head on the left, and the grassed-over spoil mountains of Central Forest Park fill the middle distance.

A long cutting now leads the Greenway through the heart of Burslem, crossed by a succession of soot-encrusted bridges of plain design. The elaborate edifice of the public baths overlooks the site of Burslem station, a wide grassy space.

The former Potteries loop line near Stoke on Trent, seen *(above)* after closure, formed a corridor traversing the industrial setting of the Six Towns and parts have been converted *(below)* into the Potteries Greenway which is seen here near Tunstall. *(H K Bowen Ltd)*

Leaving the cutting, the walker looks ahead to the ancient and modern mixture of Hanley on its hill, with a skyline of office-blocks, towers and spires. An old-fashioned bottle kiln stands in a factory yard. These small kilns, whose name describes their shape and not their product, were seen everywhere in the Six Towns a few years ago—literally a backyard industry—but nowadays they have become rare.

Cobridge station marks the limit of reclamation on the line so far, and, after the tidy pathway, it comes as a surprise to find the familiar heap of bricks, partly demolished walls and rubbish. The station bridge is filled in, and the Loop Line runs on under the shadow of the gigantic Sneyd tip, now just beginning to resemble a grassy hill, to curve round on its final run down to the main line at Etruria station.

A few minutes walk from Cobridge station site brings the walker to an appropriate place at which to finish the walk— Vale Place station in Waterloo Road, the only example of North Staffordshire Railway building still standing on the Greenway. The station building is sited, unusually, on top of the station bridge; it is a long, low, extremely plain design in dark brick, relieved only by lining in orange brick, with a wooden awning and tall, flat-topped chimneys. From the bridge, the Loop Line runs on in a rubbish-choked cutting to Etruria.

Stoke-on-Trent City Council have shown great energy and imagination in turning their motley collection of sows' ears into silk purses—and not all the sows' ears were seen as such by local people. Many felt that such features as Sneyd colliery tip were important and dramatic landmarks, which encapsulated the character and history of the city. This point of view has had to be borne in mind. The aim has been not to obliterate but to improve and incorporate the derelict sites.

But when the reclamation scheme is completed, perhaps some time in the 1980s, the continuous running-down of the Six Towns' unsightly industries will have dumped a new collection of eyesores on the city's doorstep. The Promised Land of the city of waterparks and walkways, outlined so temptingly in the reclamation programme, may remain forever beyond their grasp, but they have made an impressive start.

13 THE SPA TRAIL—
WOODHALL SPA TO
HORNCASTLE

The disused Great Northern Railway branch line runs for six miles north-east from Woodhall Spa, a peaceful haven for retired people, to the historic town of Horncastle in the Bain valley. In recognition of the variety of Lincolnshire country-side that it traverses, the former Lindsey County Council converted it to a footpath and bridleway—the 'Spa Trail'.

Woodhall Spa is a neat, quiet town with trees lining the streets. The railway runs in from Woodhall Junction, 1½ miles to the west, and crosses the main street, the Broadway, into the station site. New houses have been built here, and their well-ordered rows accompany the line as it leads out of the town along an avenue of squirrel-haunted conifers.

The Spa Trail begins officially at the large information board beside the crossing on Iddesleigh Road. A faded 'Beware of Trains' notice faces the garden gates that give onto the line. The centre of the track is untouched and over-grown, making a clear contrast to the footpath that runs beside it. The verges are dotted with harebells and bracken.

The County Council decided to forego its right to buy the mile of track that cuts through Woodhall Golf Course, and the Spa Trail makes a detour through the shaven greens and heather-covered bunkers by a wide green footpath. Many of the signposts have been uprooted, but the walker enjoys a pleasant stroll through mixed heathland and coniferous woodland. Rowan, silver birch and oak grow beside the path, and fungi sprout in the ferny ditches. Woodpeckers and chiff-chaffs call among the trees, and there are occasional glimpses of the old railway running parallel, chest-high with cow-parsley and grass. The whole area has been designated one of special scientific interest.

At Sandy Lane is the first of many signposts carrying a symbol representing a helmeted Viking's head. The Spa Trail forms part of the 'Viking Way', which will eventually run from the Humber to Oakham in Leicestershire.

The walker rejoins the line a ¼ mile down Sandy Lane, by a very plain brick crossing-keeper's cottage. The flat country-side accounts for the large number of level crossings on the branch, and the almost complete absence of bridges or major earthworks. Broom, brambles and bracken grow beside the path, which is graded for riders as well as walkers from here on. To the north west is Highall Wood, full of the shining trunks of tall birch trees, and separated from the trail by large, flat, close-cropped pasture fields. Brimstone, small copper and small white butterflies are frequently seen here.

The gates at the next crossing cottage are closed on an obliterated path. On one side trees press up against the gate, and on the other the faint tracks of cart-ruts through a corn field show where the farm track once crossed the railway. The line runs ruler-straight, sometimes on a low embank-ment, sometimes in a shallow cutting, but mostly at the level of the surrounding fields. The edge of the woods advances and recedes, and the view ahead is down a tunnel of trees as far as the eye can see. The skies seem enormous, the flat line of the horizon broken only by a gentle swell that heralds the Bain valley.

Martin picnic site is equipped with bench-and-table units of heavy wood, signposts, litter-bins and information boards. From here the trail runs on in a cutting full of elder bushes and birdsong, to pass beneath the only bridge on the line, which carries the B1191 from Woodhall to Horncastle. It is an unornamented piece of functional building in dark brick, relieved at the parapet by yellow and red brickwork where repairs have been carried out.

The line leaves the cutting and enters the wide Bain valley, with long prospects of hills in the background. Sheep graze in the coarse pasture meadows, and flocks of lapwings tumble overhead. The ruling emphasis of the flat Lincoln-shire countryside is on intensive agriculture of a highly mechanised kind.

The old railway curves north east to run the last two miles beside the old Horncastle canal, now a drainage channel for the surrounding arable land. There is irony in the situation, for the railway killed off the canal, then was overwhelmed in its turn by the petrol engine. Their enmity resolved in retirement, the two outdated antagonists wind peaceably side by side through the river valley towards the red-roofed huddle of Horncastle. Along the railway are planted young seedlings.

At Thornton Lodge Farm, the Spa Trail leaves the track beside the crossing cottage, which is painted a fresh white, in contrast to the gloomy austerity of its purple-black sisters down the branch. Opposite, in the field below the farmhouse, stands a 10ft high cylinder of grass-grown red brick—the reservoir tower of the farm's old well.

The walk continues into Horncastle along the canal bank, reached by a concrete bridge a few yards to the east of the level-crossing. The tow-path passes a derelict lock, with cable-operated paddles and the gates missing. Though disused, the canal is clear enough of weed for fish to be seen swimming in the foot or so of water. A bridge crosses the canal on the outskirts of Horncastle, leading the walker by a narrow path into the market town, once famed for its horse fair—the biggest in the world, but now just a memory.

Beside the path stands Horncastle station, the terminus of the short branch line. The sturdy, four-square station building well repays a visit. Used nowadays by an agricultural firm and surrounded by machinery, its red-brick solidity is still impressive. There are six windows on the frontage of the upper storey, once the stationmaster's residence, and curlicued decoration over the door. The hipped roof carries tall chimneys, and the south end of the building is extended to include the offices. The Great Northern Railway was often accused of ugly functionalism in building; this station is certainly functional, but dignified and strong as well.

At the entrance to the station yard is an old notice-board, now split into its component strakes, on which is nailed in raised letters:

'L.N.E.R. SPEED OF MOTORS NOT TO EXCEED
3 MILES PER HOUR'

On a shed door is a ripped and faded poster, headed:

'Closing of Freight Depot.
Horncastle and Woodhall Junction.'

14 THE WIRRAL COUNTRY PARK

The Wirral peninsula pokes its blunt snout north west into Liverpool Bay, between the shoulders of industrial Merseyside and North Wales. The land is flat, split between Liverpool's dormitory towns and large, bare fields.

On the north eastern shore of the peninsula are grouped Liverpool's subsidiary districts, Wallasey and Birkenhead. They are separated from the parent city by the narrow estuary of the River Mersey, though their present-day commuters can burrow deep under the river via the sub-aqueous tunnels and be in Liverpool five minutes later.

Travelling in the opposite direction, one leaves the extraordinary city centre of Liverpool, where an intricate, curling road system carries the driver indiscriminately past buildings straight out of classical Athens, crumbling red brick derelicts, seagull-frequented advertisement hoardings and windy gaps between the office tower blocks. After the long, dimly-lit plunge and climb of the Queensway Tunnel, Birkenhead seems much more archetypally Liverpudlian than Liverpool itself. Here are the expected steep, cobbled streets of dark terraced houses, face to face; the drab, stained bus shelters; the dismal 1950s council blocks of flats. But as the clanging Mersey is left behind and the influence of urban Liverpool begins to fade, another character emerges—low, rolling agricultural land, with smaller towns and quiet country lanes. This is the Wirral proper, where in spite of the new administrative designation of 'Merseyside', the inhabitants feel themselves part of Cheshire, and independent, if not positively scornful, of Liverpool.

The south western face of the Wirral peninsula looks out across the estuary of the River Dee. Less than ten miles from the Mersey, the Dee has a completely different atmosphere.

Instead of the bustle and clamour of industrial dockland, here are salt marshes and mud flats, where shore birds gather to feed in the quiet margins of the estuary—curlew, dunlin and oystercatchers, which probe the marshy ground for cockles and mussels. The broad, flat river gives a sense of space and openness to the sky. Sailing boats skim up and down the estuary, and anglers, walkers and riders have room for their activities. Perhaps the greatest contrast is in the view across the two rivers. In the north east, tower blocks, cranes and warehouses dominate the skyline, pressing in on the crowded Mersey and making it seem even narrower than it is. On the other side of the peninsula, one looks out across the wide Dee to a flat, peaceful shore, backed by the blue hills of North Wales.

The railways came early to this part of England. George Stephenson's Stockton & Darlington Railway, opened in 1825, was primarily concerned in its pioneer years with goods traffic. Stephenson was soon at work building the first railway to be properly timetabled for both goods and passenger traffic, between Liverpool and Manchester. It opened in 1830 and the inhabitants of Lancashire and Cheshire soon became accustomed to the busy engines and clanking trucks, feeding the major centres with goods and transporting the citizens at hitherto undreamed-of speeds.

For more than thirty years the fishing ports and farming villages of south west Wirral remained in their previous isolation. Then the sound of high explosive echoed across the quiet waters of the Dee as the railway navvies blasted a path through the red sandstone rock. Embankments rose, bridges spanned the cuttings, station buildings appeared on the outskirts of small towns. The modern world was muscling-in on the farmers and fishermen. Down went the ballast, sleepers and rails of a single-track branch line from Hooton in the south east to West Kirby in the north west. By 1886 the whole twelve miles was complete.

The Wirral branch line gave access to Liverpool from West Kirby, and to Chester from Hooton. In its early years it was owned jointly by the London & North Western and Great Western railways. Each company had to emphasise its own identity in the joint venture, while co-operating with its partner. Until the first world war, trains were either LNWR or GWR. After the war, perhaps compelled to a more catholic attitude by wartime stringencies, trains of mixed parentage were run by the GWR and its partners the LNWR until 1923, and the London, Midland & Scottish after the 1923 amalgamation. The GWR, true to its usual branch line policy, used only tank engines on the line, but in later years the occasional LMS Stanier Class 5 4-6-0 or other large mixed traffic locomotive might be routed via the branch.

The railway staff seem to have been well mixed from the beginning, though the buildings themselves, at the south eastern end of the line, showed a strong LNWR influence. Each station had its share of characters on the staff: Mr Peacock, the signalman at Heswall, who festooned his signal-box with geraniums and ferns; the three men at one time working at Hadlow Road station, quite unrelated to each other, who shared the surname Davies and whose Christian names were Tom, Dick and Harry; and the bearded signal-man with the gammy leg at Parkgate, Mr Sam Worral, a great favourite with the boys from the nearby Mostyn House School. According to one account, 'On being released from Mostyn House School we would run up to the station and if it was a wet and windy night would seek shelter in Sam's box and warm ourselves at his fire. Depending on his mood at the time we were either made welcome or Sam would seize a signal flag and shout "Get out you little . . . s or I'll prattle your arses with a stick." More often than not we got a welcome and a warm by the fire.'

The railways were sensitive to the possibilities of attracting well-to-do customers, of whom there was no shortage. On the 8 o'clock train from Heswall, an important businessman's service, an LNWR 'club' carriage was provided for the big-wigs, with armchair seats and bridge tables—though the Mostyn House schoolboy quoted above, together with his friends, was 'pushed into the third class carriages'. The rail-way was undoubtedly responsible for spreading a thick layer of commuters along the Wirral peninsula. It also provided the usual boost to the local economy, as farmers and fisher-men found they could get their products further in larger quantities. Ten-ton wagonloads of potatoes for planting came in by train. Traffic through Birkenhead and Wallasey docks used the line to reach the main railway network. The

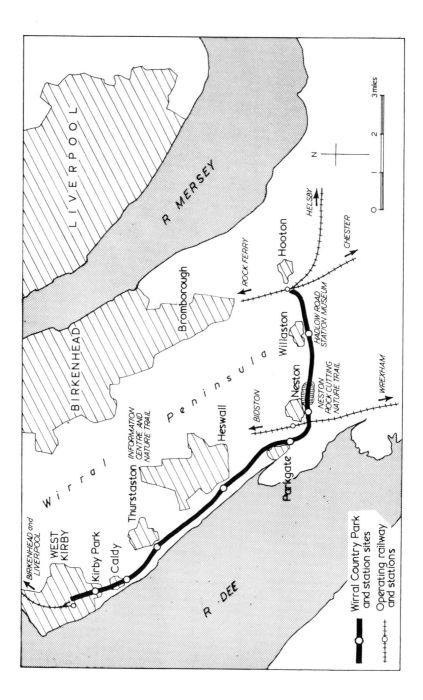

natives themselves travelled further afield, and came back with new goods, new fashions, new ideas.

Railway companies came and went; staff changed with the years; Mr Pye of Heswall started a rival bus service during a railway strike; but the line continued in much the same peaceful way until the 1950s. Then the familiar pattern set in—declining passenger and goods usage; the growth of individual motoring, luring holidaymakers away from the secluded pleasures of Parkgate and Heswall to more adventurous Blackpool and Llandudno; the slow, sure strangulation as the timetable shed its services. On 15 September, 1956, the Wirral branch lost its passengers. In 1962 goods trains also ceased to run, and eventually the track was lifted.

The drains that ran under the cuttings became choked and overflowed along the line. Some bridges were dismantled, leaving only their dressed stone abutments flanking the roads. Brambles and gorse grew unchecked on the trackbed. The station buildings crumbled into decay. British Railways began to sell off portions of the track. The railway was dead.

Or was it?

On 3 April, 1968, Cheshire County Council produced a report, 'Cheshire Countryside—a scheme for a Wirral Country Park'. It opened by quoting a statement made by the Minister of Land and Natural Resources to the 'Countryside in 1970' conference, held in November 1965:

> They (Country Parks) would make it easier for people to enjoy their leisure in the open without travelling too far and adding to the congestion on the roads; and by concentrating the more gregarious activities in particular places, they would reduce the risk that visitors (and their cars) would sprawl all over the place, to the annoyance of farmers, landowners and residents in the country and, indeed, of the visitors themselves.

The report pointed out that Merseyside and Wirral together contained a population of a million and a half, which could be expected to have reached 1,800,000 within the next twenty-five years. Provision for countryside recreation was quite insufficient for this enormous and rapidly increasing number of people. The report recommended that a Wirral Country Park should be established to cater for the present and future recreational needs of Merseyside and Wirral, based on the abandoned Hooton to West Kirby railway line.

The County Council was urged to buy all the available remaining land from British Railways. The total cost of the scheme was estimated at £223,500–£243,500 (roughly half of this in buying the land); maintenance costs would start at £2,000 a year, and rise after the opening of the park to £15,000 a year. The report then examined the scheme in detail, taking the line section by section.

The report represented the fruits of several years' cautious inquiry by Cheshire County Council. The idea of setting up a country park on the line had been discussed since withdrawal of passenger services in 1956. While bricks and mortar fell apart at Thurstaston station, and Neston rock cutting was marked down for a rubbish tip, the bureaucratic machine turned the idea over. While the few remaining windows at Hadlow Road were smashed, and farmers fenced off the track, the country park began to take shape—on paper. Finally, the local authority machine flashed on 'green for go', and regurgitated its report. The 1960s were rich with hope for new, imaginative schemes, which was fortunate for the infant country park, for had the machine taken a few more years to make up its mind, the dead hand of 'economy measures' would surely have choked off its product at the report stage, if not before. As it was, the Countryside Commission gave its approval, thereby releasing grant money. The Wirral Country Park, under the overall management of Cheshire County Council, could move off the drawing-board on to the ground.

At the same time, Major Frank White was looking around for a countryside job with challenge. Active and energetic, he had retired prematurely from the Army. Cheshire County Council selected him from well over a thousand applicants for the position of Head Ranger of the Wirral Country Park. For the first few weeks, Major White camped out in an old station building and took stock of his formidable task. Then he set to work.

On a bleak winter's morning in 1976, I arrived at the Visitor Centre at Thurstaston station to spend the day on the Wirral

Country Park with Frank White. A bitter wind was whipping stinging flurries of sleet across the Dee estuary, and mud squelched underfoot. Round the trim stone buildings of the Visitor Centre, the park rangers in their green weatherproofs were busy with Land Rovers and trailers. A heap of freshly made wooden signboards lay ready to be put into position along the park. Even in this freezing weather, the rangers have their capable hands full with hedging and ditching, fence maintenance, litter collection and a thousand and one other routine outdoor jobs. In winter they reckon to spend 70 per cent of their time on maintenance work, and the rest on caring for the visitors; in summer, of course, season of tourists and holidaymakers, the proportions are reversed.

In the main building is laid out an explanatory exhibition—the drawings, photographs and notes that one might expect, plus an historical progression, geological, geographical and naturalistic, of the story of the Wirral peninsula. Red sandstone Triassic rocks rub shoulders with stuffed and mounted animals typical of those found on the park—foxes, badgers, hedgehogs, weasels, winter-coated stoats. An automatically operated illuminated slide show tells the story of the branch line, and introduces the various attractions of the park. In summer, live examples of pond-dwelling creatures are exhibited in small tanks, let into a display board. This is an imaginative way to inform not only the casual visitors, but also the school parties which come to the park. According to Frank White, the children usually congregate fascinated in front of an ingenious working model which demonstrates with swirling water and sand how the Dee estuary has silted up over the centuries.

Upstairs, the full extent of the park's achievement is demonstrated in a series of 'before and after' photographs. The 'before' photographs show derelict, rubble-strewn stations, flooded cuttings and ugly mountains of rubbish. Gradually, the ideas of the 1968 report took shape. Bulldozers moved in to flatten out the pits and mounds. Volunteers set about the enormous, monotonous job of grubbing out the brambles and undergrowth. Forgotten drains and culverts were painstakingly tracked down, re-opened and cleaned out.

Once the main physical obstacles were cleared away,

103

planning for the future could start. Quite apart from the problems posed by site clearance and the provision of amenities for visitors, there were diplomatic exercises to be carried out. Even allowing for the long-drawn-out negotiations which are the norm where purchase of railway land is concerned, twelve years is a long time for land to lie untenanted; the newly appointed park rangers under Frank White found considerable opposition to the very idea of the park, from those who had either bought sections of track, or whose property abutted the old line. Would a country park bring hordes of vandals, smashing up fences and lighting fires? How could rangers guarantee the privacy of houses backing onto the line? Moreover, did the Wirral really want an invasion by the type of city-dwelling recreation seeker, ignorant of the country, greedy for pinball tables and bags of chips, who might be going to try out the park? Frank White set himself and his rangers the primary task of establishing good relations with their new neighbours.

The park had to prove itself an asset rather than a nuisance to the Wirral coast, fitting in unobtrusively yet announcing its existence boldly, thereby attracting enough patrons to justify the time, money and effort put into its creation. It had to offer the kinds of amenities and safeguards which people had come to expect of town-based leisure centres, yet provide a simpler, more informal environment in which to enjoy countryside activities. It had to cater for the academic botanist, the historian and the day tripper. Cheshire County Council, having laboured long to bring forth its project, was anxious to see it brought to fruition within the brief set by the Minister of Land and Natural Resources in 1965. Between all these conflicting interests the staff of the country park have walked a tightrope, occasionally wobbling but keeping all parties satisfied, thanks largely to the energy and dedication of the head ranger, who mediates in the event of a serious clash of interests.

Two small examples of adjustment between the park and its neighbours illustrate this balance. Sections of the park used by those on foot and those on horseback are segregated in most places by a post-and-rail fence. At Caldy, a mile or so along the line from West Kirby, a certain householder found that the much-prized view from his favourite chair by

104

the picture window, across the Dee estuary to the Welsh hills, was obscured by the horizontal rail. A few words with the head ranger, a dip of a few inches in the height of the rail at the strategic point—satisfaction on both sides. Almost next door, another resident found the view too much for him; riders were getting grandstand glimpses through his first floor windows. A screen of bushy saplings was planted on the bank, and privacy returned. A less readily resolved difficulty at this spot was with Caldy Golf Club, beside whose course the old line runs, and whose members took some convincing that the park users would not encroach onto their carefully kept greens.

One of the great attractions of basing the country park on the old railway was the linear nature of the track. For walkers and riders, it was vital to provide an uninterrupted right of way over the whole twelve miles. But even after the line was bought from British Railways there were breaks in the continuity of the railway at three places. The stations at Heswall and Neston South had already been purchased for housing development, so short detours were necessary at these points. Between Neston and Willaston, at the south eastern end of the railway, the University of Liverpool veterinary field station had bought the line as an underpass to connect its teaching area and isolation unit with its experimental farm. This privacy had to be respected, but at the time it looked as if users of the country park would have to make a detour via a busy main road. Cheshire County Council kept negotiations under way, however, and was finally rewarded with access permission by way of the hitherto forbidden underpass.

While overall continuity was being established, some of the broken bridges were replaced with wooden spans. Others had their stone abutments demolished, and the sheer faces each side of the road smoothed out into a gentle gradient. Old fencing was mended and new fencing erected. At the extremities of the park, West Kirby and Hooton, shrubs, trees and hedges were planted to screen the industrial scene. Elsewhere on the park more planting was carried out to lessen the formality of rows of houses, to break up and enliven dull views, and to give the residents privacy. Slowly, with many checks and changes of plan, the shabby, overgrown old railway line disappeared, and the Wirral Country Park emerged—chrysalis to butterfly.

Looking at the park from the visitor's point of view on that biting winter day, I could hardly recognize some of the scenes of dereliction in the 'before' photographs on display at Thurstaston Visitor Centre. The neat buildings of the centre are separated from the estuary foreshore by a chain of rounded hillocks, to all appearances shaped by centuries of salty breezes and tidal erosion. But under their short turf lie the hideous remains of a wartime gun site—now the grim grey blocks and bricks are hidden away under earth and grass.

Further on are ponds where anglers can buy a cheap permit and try their luck for rudd, tench, carp and gudgeon. Other ponds are set aside for specialist study of aquatic life—the Thurstaston Nature Reserve check list gives, like Heinz, 57 varieties. Yet a few short years ago these teeming ponds were crumbling, abandoned marl pits, from which the Thurstaston farmers had once dug out clay with a 10 per cent lime content, good enough to fertilise their heavy soil. When artificial fertilisers came into general use, the marl holes were left to decay, until rehabilitated and stocked by those who saw further than their ugly uselessness.

While the administration of the Park centres on Thurstaston, the other station sites have also been put to good use. There are picnic areas and lavatories, information centres and car parks, for almost all visitors come by car. From the site at Parkgate, the visitor can explore the fascinating small town. Here the tidal Dee used to flow right up against the sea wall, a few feet from the houses. The wide, slow-moving Dee never generated the vigorous scouring energy of the narrower Mersey, and rising banks of silt far inland put an end to Chester as a commercial port four hundred years ago. For three centuries Parkgate, nearer the estuary mouth, grew fat on the proceeds of Chester's losses—then was hoist with a delayed-action petard of the same nature. Now sea wall stands in isolation, facing well over a mile of mud flats, saltings and spartina grass. Geese and snipe come here in numbers, and water-rail can sometimes be seen running along the sea-road. A stone-built quay, once loud with sailors' oaths and the creak of wooden fishing boats, juts out into the spartina, redundant. The boys from Mostyn House School, when not plaguing Sam Worral in his signal box, built a stone swimming bath by the sea wall, which filled with salt water at high tide—but no bathers will congregate along its flaking sides again. In the narrow, twisting streets of Parkgate, pub names hold seafaring memories—*The Greenland Fisheries*—but tourists and commuters drink there nowadays. Imperceptibly, the fickle, shallow river has slunk away, building up wider and wider margins between itself and its former associates.

The shores of South Wirral and North Wales are getting closer all the time. Impatient Man, however, cannot wait for nature to do the bridge-building, but has planned a huge dam-cum-road, linking Merseyside and North Wales across the mouth of the Dee. The fact that he will thereby upset the delicate ecological balance, the tidal systems and the micro-climate, endangering hundreds of bird, plant and sea-creature species, seems of no account compared with the needs of the great gods Commerce and Convenience.

Two places on the park are of special interest. One is Hadlow Road station, which has been carefully restored to look as it might have done on a normal working day in 1952. From the outside, one sees a simple LNWR type building. Brightly coloured enamel advertisements for Bovril and Hudson's Soap adorn the red and black brick walls below plain, slate roofs. Inside, the ticket office and booking hall wait in suspended animation for the next train from Hooton. Here is all the railway paraphernalia a fanatic could desire— ticket press and date stamp, elaborate travel posters, luggage scales and stationmaster's special chair in front of the fire. From a photograph taken in the 1930s, the staff stare down, no doubt itching to make tea in the preserved enamel jug, and straighten up the bundles of books and papers on the desk. On the platform, the station trolley bears a load of milk churns and a schoolboy's tuck-box.

The other place of special interest is a long, deep cutting through the sandstone on the eastern outskirts of Neston. This section has been made the subject of a separate nature trail, as it contains several intriguing features. As the walker descends the long slope into the cutting, the cool damp air trapped at the bottom wraps a chilly blanket round his feet,

Above: The Waverley route from Carlisle to Edinburgh running right across the Southern Uplands of Scotland was one of the main lines closed to all traffic in the 1960s; much of it ran through moorland and since closure the trackbed has returned to nature. *(John Goss)*
Right: The Wirral Country Park has been created out of the route of the former GW/LNW joint line from Hooton to West Kirby. This is the remarkable Neston rock cutting, a nature trail where walkers now pass where trains once ran. *(Graham Hutt)*

then works its way up to numb the rest of his body. This must have been a hellish place for the railway navvies to work, camped in crude shelters with little chance of ever getting thoroughly dry. All along the sheer walls can be seen the short, diagonal scars of their pickaxe blows as they forged a way through the sandstone. Every so often appear the round shot-holes in which the dynamite was lodged before detonation. Halfway along the cutting, the date 1866 is scored deeply into the rock—probably the year the cutting was excavated. Above it appears the date 1964. Frank White guesses that this was left behind by the gang which dismantled the track after closure.

From the botanist's point of view, the most interesting feature of the cutting is that the land through which it was made has a general slope from the south in a downward direction towards the north. Water drains into the cutting along the south wall, and away from it to the north, resulting in a permanently damp south wall and dry north wall. Liverworts, mosses and ferns grow in lush profusion on the damp wall, matted with icicles that frozen day, while lichens and spiders' webs have the north wall pretty much to themselves. In a recent survey, 115 plant species were counted in the cutting, of which only twenty-five were common to both sides—a happy divide for the botanically minded. The mellifluous names listed in the Neston rock cutting nature trail guide constitute a herbal poetry in themselves—creeping bent-grass, sheep's fescue and Yorkshire fog, greater stitchwort, hawkweed, hogweed, soft rush and wild carrot, to name a handful.

Geologically, too, the cutting is rich: 200-million-year-old Bunter Pebble Bed Triassic sandstone forms the walls. There are clearly displayed examples of faults—contorted, folded sandwiches of twisted rock, buckled up under immense pressure—all exposed by the navvies' picks a century ago, and carefully cleaned by the rangers.

The guide calls the visitor's attention to wrens, blackbirds, song thrushes, willow warblers and chiff-chaffs, all of which frequent the cutting, while the last few pages are taken up with monstrous, science-fiction freaks, bristling with legs and jaws—six-inch blow-ups of woodlice and centipedes. A footnote says, reassuringly, 'The specimens shown in the drawings are greatly enlarged.'

The Neston rock cutting is a natural treasure house. Today's visitor to the Wirral Country Park can count himself lucky that it is still there for him to enjoy. At the time of the 1968 report, a trunk sewer pipe was already in position along the floor of the cutting. Neston UDC then proposed to fill in the cutting nearly to the top with refuse. After pressure from the Country Park planners, the tipping scheme was abandoned. The sewer pipe remains, accompanying the walker through the cutting at a height of about three feet. Manhole covers stick up at chest height. As a disguise for this functional but aesthetically displeasing item, mosses have been

Two scenes in the Wirral Country Park. *Above:* The former Hooton–West Kirby line ran along the shore of the Dee estuary, and the country park takes in not only the railway route but also a derelict former World War II gun emplacement with its attendant buildings and a flooded marl pit which has now been landscaped. *(Graham Hutt) Below:* Wild flowers and hedgerows now border the former railway route and offer the walker an idyllic setting to get away from it all. *(Graham Hutt)*

encouraged to grow on the concrete sheath which encases the pipe. The manhole covers were wrapped in turf, which it is hoped will 'take', to give them a more natural outline. In fact one visitor, on being asked by a ranger what he thought the manhole covers contained, hazarded a guess at charcoal burners' ovens!

Without the efforts of the country park management, the cool echoing cutting with its dates, pick marks and wild life would almost certainly be under several feet of rubbish by now.

The summer season naturally sees the park at its most popular; but over a whole year half a million visitors are expected. The small force of rangers has to be very efficiently organised to cope with such a large number, and it is not surprising to find a distinctly military flavour about their operations. At least 500 applications are made for each post of ranger, and the six men chosen, together with another six part-timers, make up a tough, experienced staff with a surprisingly wide variety of backgrounds and personal specialist interests. They are charged with every duty from first aid to fence maintenance. They keep their eyes open for new foxes' earths or wild flowers, advise and educate the visitors, and clean up after them. The rangers have to be prepared for duty until any hour of day or night, and their pay bears no relation whatever to their dedication and the quality of their work.

In all, the Wirral Country Park represents a triumph for its creators, and a good example for other local authorities to follow. The success of the whole venture can be gauged by the reaction of the local chapter of the Hell's Angels when they came to give the park the once-over. Despite trepidation on the part of the staff, the Angels enjoyed the atmosphere so much that their leader told Frank White that they intended to add the country park to their list of outings— 'Bloody lovely!'

Perhaps the most significant sign has been given by the residents of West Kirby whose houses skirt the old railway. When the park was first planned, they clamoured for wire fences and chains to keep the invaders out of their gardens. Nowadays the demand is for gates to be built into their garden fences to allow the residents *onto* the park.

15 THE 'BISHOP–BRANDON WALK'—DURHAM TO BISHOP AUCKLAND

This ten-mile path through a famous coal-mining area was created by Durham County Council along the track of the branch line opened in 1857 from Leamside to Bishop Auckland via Durham City. The 'Bishop–Brandon Walk' is remarkable for the different types of countryside through which it runs—sweeping views of distant hills, huddled and noisy mining villages, and isolated farmsteads. Only in one part does the constant noise of heavy traffic and machinery fade into the background. But the charm of the walk lies in the glimpses the walker has of the varied facets that make up the character of County Durham.

The walk starts at Neville's Cross on the western outskirts of Durham. The Lanchester Valley Walk, another council scheme established on the old railway from Durham to Consett, runs away north west from the main line by a bridge over the B6302. On the other side of the bridge, the walker descends to the Bishop Auckland line through a waymarked stile. The walk follows a wide, clear path along the embankment, surfaced with black ash which soon makes its mark on the shins. The views are enormous, rolling downland on far horizons, with the red rows of pit villages dotted everywhere.

The path dips down to the little River Deerness to avoid the site of a demolished viaduct. The banks are already thickly grassed and flowery; in a few years' time they will be indistinguishable from natural hillocks. On the sheltered stretches of track are young nursery trees—mountain ash, beeches, sycamore and spruce—planted in compost beds beside the path. Plain wooden stiles allow the walker passage over fences across the track.

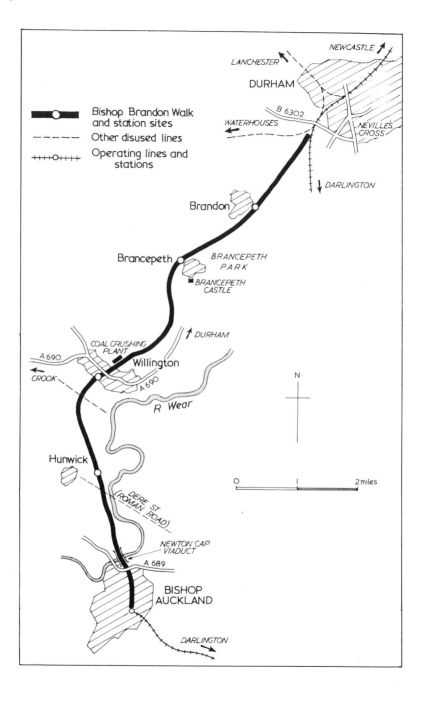

Entering the large mining village of Brandon, the track skirts an open green, then in contrast a National Coal Board tip, a hellish area of waste ground and sprawling coal heaps; an eye-sore in the heart of the village. A chipped enamel notice warns off illicit coal-pickers, but locals, undaunted, fill their barrows gratis from the tip's plentiful supply.

Further from the path is the first indication that the walk has railway connections—a rusty, faded sign:

DANGEROUS CROSSING 30 YDS AHEAD

Station Avenue runs beside the track, but only a stretch of crushed red bricks underfoot shows where Brandon station once stood. A long cutting, with clover underfoot and toadflax and coltsfoot on the banks, leads the path out of Brandon through wooded fields. Hazel and willow are beginning to colonise the trackside scrub, being colonised themselves by crowds of finches.

The straggling mining village is soon left behind, and the long spaces of Brancepeth Park lie alongside, with low hills ahead. Between the trees—healthy, full-crowned elms—are views of the Georgian estate village of Brancepeth, with honey-coloured houses on tree-lined roads. The track passes through a shallow cutting, a secluded spot which reflects the character of the estate. The overbridges on the rest of the line are of sturdy, workmanlike design, but here they are embellished with delicate cornicing, light and fine by comparison. Heather blooms thickly on the cutting sides, and harebells dot the clover with blue.

Brancepeth station, inhabited and immaculately maintained, also forsakes red brick in favour of a neo-Georgian design in stone the colour of clotted cream, with two deep ornamented gables facing the track, and a big, heavy old railway clock still fixed to the wall. An iron North Eastern Railway notice, half smothered under ivy, admonishes trespassers on the railway.

A tall embankment, lined with sycamores, takes the path away from the station, with the towers and battlements of Brancepeth Castle appearing on a promontory above Stockley Beck. Beyond the borders of the park, the cornicing on the bridges disappears, and there are wide views again from the track. Bare fields run on each side, with wind-blown stone outbuildings crouched round the farmhouses.

The Bishop Brandon walk from Bishop Auckland to Brandon and the outskirts of Durham has been converted by Durham County Council into a bridleway and footpath with much cleaning up needed at certain places along the route as can be seen in these before and after photographs. *(County Planning Department, Durham County Council)*

Not all of the route between Bishop Auckland and Durham has been retained for walkers and this viaduct just outside Durham was demolished, forcing walkers to detour from one side of the valley to the other. *(County Planning Department, Durham County Council)*

Ahead is the untidy outline of the former mining settlement of Willington, dominated from the track by a mighty coal-crushing plant. In other days the coal came from Willington pits to be broken down, but now lorries bring it from far afield. Different grades of coal are produced here, from coarse chips down to the fine powder used in blast-furnaces.

The original miners' houses in the village are built of dull buff-and-black stone, and run in stepped terraces up the hillside. From the path the walker can compare these relics of private ownership with the bright new orange roofs of the recent developments. The old railway has been integrated into the village as an arterial footpath, provided with ornamental trees, benches and lighting.

A sign, hand painted with many flourishes on the end wall of a terrace, advertises to long-dead railway travellers a real Jack-of-all-trades:

J.H. ARMORY
BUILDING CONTRACTOR
JOINER   CABINET MAKER
& UNDERTAKER
PAINTER   PLUMBER

Beyond the busy streets of the village, the grassy track of the walk crosses over the grassy track of the branch line which ran up to Crook Town. Other tramway tracks can be picked out, leading to pits that have long ceased to operate. Dere Street Roman road, now a green lane, slants across the path; and ahead the houses of Bishop Auckland are piled one above another. This small market town looks down on the meandering River Wear. There is still a thriving market, and many old-fashioned steep cobbled terrace streets by the river, the majority of their houses derelict and boarded-up. The walk approaches Bishop Auckland over a tall twelve-arched viaduct across the Wear, which the council has thankfully retained. There is a stunning, if vertiginous, view from its centre up the river and down onto the old road bridge at the edge of the town.

The short tunnel which led the line into Bishop Auckland station is bricked up, and the Bishop–Brandon Walk ends with a climb up into the sloping streets of the old town.

118

16 THE PENCAITLAND RAILWAY WALK—SMEATON TO WEST SALTOUN

The mines of the East Lothian coalfield are, or were, many and far-flung. All the small ones have closed by now, finding the struggle for survival too much for them. But in Victorian days there were handfuls of shoe-string pits round each town, producing a few hundred tons a day and giving employment to a few hundred able-bodied local men.

The Pencaitland railway walk, created in 1971 by the then East Lothian County Council, is based on a section of the railway line which linked up those pits between the Edinburgh suburb of Dalkeith and the village of Gifford at the foot of the Lammermuir Hills.

It is possible to join the track at Smeaton, just outside Dalkeith, but the line, running in a deep, overgrown cutting, has a stream flowing down the middle, the result of choked drains and culverts. This western end of the railway runs through waterlogged marshland, rich in reeds, watermint and sedges, with large cornfields sweeping up to the sky-line. The official five-mile walk starts near the village of Elphinstone.

The rangers employed on the walk have been busy penning back the strong undergrowth, surfacing the track with finely crushed cinders, and erecting information boards which carry a large replica of the hand written and drawn guide produced by the county planning department. The walking is easy and pleasant, with an intriguing mixture all round of open, cultivated but unfrequented cornfields, strewn with the harsh outlines of abandoned colliery buildings, and slag-heaps with deep rain-water channels in their flanks like miniature Alps. The buildings are mostly of mottled grey and pink firebrick, and the soil thrown up around the pit-heaps makes a sharp contrast to the bright yellow corn, its dark colour betraying the presence of coal.

Short spurs run from the track among the ruins. The mines gave birth to the railway, built in 1867 by the North British Railway as far as Ormiston, primarily as an outlet for coal, with passenger traffic very much a subsidiary benefit. East Lothian County Council has acknowledged the influence of the mines by erecting what at first sight appear to be grave-stones opposite the sites of former pits, each stone engraved with a few details.

'Oxenford Pit (Ormiston Coal Co.). Sunk 1907. Re-sunk 1909. Abandoned 1932. Output before closure 250/300 tons a day.'

'Woodhall Pit. (Woodhall Coal Co.). Sunk 1852. Not fully exploited until 1904. Abandoned 1944. 198 men employed (in) 1943.'

They paint a laconic picture of a multitude of tiny pits—thirteen at least on this five mile stretch of line—worked by small-time companies who set up as and when they could, and disappeared without trace when the coal did. The grave-stones reveal that most of the pits worked different parts of the same seams, whose curious names crop up over and over again: Five Feet, Four Feet and Three Feet, Ball No 1 and No 2, Splint, Parrot and Diamond.

Near Ormiston, marsh is replaced by grassland, inter-spersed with more cornfields. Long avenues of broom bushes line the track, their dried black seed pods whispering and crackling restlessly. In the distance rise the pale blue Lammermuir Hills.

Ormiston station buildings have gone without trace, but picnic bench-and-table units are set on the platforms, and visitors can camp here. Two old lattice-work signals guard the entrances, with LNER bulls-eye lamps still in position. The North British Railway was content to halt its line at Ormiston, but in 1901 it was extended to Gifford, at the high cost of £100,000, by the Gifford & Garvald Light Railway Company.

The railway walk continues from Ormiston through a pleasant stretch of wooded country, curving south and west, alternating between embankments giving wide views over the surrounding farmland, and cuttings whose sides are thick with gorse, haws, blackthorn and more clumps of broom. Railway relics are few: an iron post which once held a warning sign, an old gradient marker engraved 'LEVEL:50', a concrete sleeper upright in the bank, with the oval imprint of a chair still visible.

At the site of Pencaitland station, huge galvanised grain silos tower in serried ranks above the line. A broken bridge over a side road has been replaced with a new wooden span. The railway walk leads on through more lonely woodland, with glimpses of tall mine chimneys between the trees, and down a steep bank to terminate at West Saltoun station. The wooden station building is still standing on a rotting wooden platform, used nowadays as a brucellosis testing station. Another lattice-work signal marks the end of the Pencaitland railway walk. In front of the platform, a venerable lady lies forlornly on the ground—an ancient all-wooden passenger coach which dates from near the birth of the railway. Her windows and doorways are blank with boards. Her sister lies in the garden beyond. Although the railway was not closed to freight until 1964, passenger services were withdrawn as long ago as 1933. Perhaps these old twins have lain at West Saltoun station since then.

The verdict on the railway in the Walk Guide is that it was 'conceived too late, was poorly planned and badly run'. None of these criticisms apply to the Pencaitland railway walk, which makes a very enjoyable introduction to the hills of Southern Scotland.

17 CONCLUSION

Over the last fifteen years, leisure activities in Britain have assumed an importance which they have never had before. Most city dwellers have accepted as one of their basic rights the provision of opportunities for sporting activities and open air exercise of all kinds. But one need in particular is increasing at a faster rate than it can be met by sporting and athletic societies—the need for long continuous miles of open space where the individual can simply roam at will, with no set object in mind.

I have tried to show how the priceless asset of the old railway network can meet this need. As areas of countryside untouched by urban influence are whittled away, the recreational potential of disused lines, their therapeutic and educational value, becomes more and more evident.

The main threat to the old railway system is the passage of time. While local authorities will not buy, and owners (including British Railways) will not sell or dedicate the derelict tracks, their condition continues to deteriorate year by year. The Golden Age is now; enough time has elapsed since the era of Dr Beeching and his axe for wildlife to have re-established itself, without rubbish and brambles accumulating to the point where conversion projects would be too difficult and expensive. Appendix A lists most of the old railways which have been converted to footpaths and bridleways, and those conversions which are planned for the future. But more action is needed. At a time of financial cutbacks it would be unrealistic to expect much of a local authority's budget to go towards such projects. But disused railways pass through almost every county, which could at the very least be earmarked for future development.

Why should local authorities not recruit volunteers in universities, schools and youth organisations to prepare the ground and hold back the advance of scrub and rubbish until money is less tight? Many organisations specialise in the care of old buildings, and in studying and preserving wildlife and plants. There are surely enough interested people here to be given a brief to take on the maintenance of these aspects of old railways. Of course, the major works—safety of bridges, viaducts and tunnels, drainage and trackbed renovation— would have to be left to the experts. But concern for the disappearing open spaces is growing all the time; people are willing to help if given a lead. British Railways might find out before closing a line whether local bodies would help to stop the disgraceful decay of so many marvellous buildings, and keep the track clear of undergrowth if the line remains unsold. The Countryside Commission is concentrating its concern on footpaths and bridleways—grant money for the basic maintenance of the old railways by voluntary groups would double their number of paths. Farmers might consider before returning strips of disused track to agricultural use that as footpaths they would keep ramblers on one predictable route, and off crops and fields. There might still be scope for work to be undertaken under Government job creation scheme grants.

Prompt action is needed. We have on our doorsteps stimulation for the naturalist, the historian, the school party, the solitary walker. It is delightful to walk on a level green path past the flower-decked shapes of old platforms between butterfly-haunted banks—not so pleasant to emerge from a bloody battle with a thorn-choked cutting to find a heap of smashed-up bricks. There is a real danger of the old railway lines, with all their possibilities, being lost to us for ever.

If you, patient reader, find you have itchy feet after reading this book, then get your boots on and go and see for yourself.

APPENDIX A
Converted Lines in England, Scotland and Wales

The following county-by-county and borough-by-borough list is as complete as it can be at the time of going to press and is based on information supplied by London boroughs and county councils in England, Scotland and Wales. The Countryside Commission compiled a list in 1970 of the situation at that time; since then many new conversion projects have been started or planned, while the reorganisation of local government and current economic circumstances have caused others to be shelved or abandoned.

Those marked **X** have been completed and opened to the public. Those marked **O** are either in hand, or are planned in the short or long term.

England—Counties

AVON

    1 **X** Lyncombe Vale, Bath. Linear Park on short stretch of Somerset & Dorset Railway line, between Devonshire and Combe Down tunnels. Also used as Nature Study area. (See Chapter 6, page 55.)

    2 **O** Footpath (2 miles) from Radstock to Midsomer Norton along S&D track.

BEDFORDSHIRE

    3 **X** Nature trail and picnic site along Stevington railway line.

BUCKINGHAMSHIRE

4 **X** Wolverton–Newport Pagnell branch. A footpath linking the citywide footpath and cycleway system at Milton Keynes. Renovation scheme in progress, involving surfacing of the route, street lighting, connections to adjacent sites and provision of seats. Future proposals include extending the walk at each end, and seats and picnic areas at former station sites.

CHESHIRE

5 **X** The Whitegate Way. Footpath and bridleway west of Winsford, central Cheshire. Car park, toilets and picnic site at Whitegate station.

CLEVELAND

6 **O** East Cleveland walkway system from Nunthorpe through Guisborough to North Skelton and Brotton.

7 **O** Eston–Normanby Walkway. To be fully developed and landscaped.

8 **O** Castle Eden walkway and bridleway from Bowesfield Junction, Stockton-on-Tees, north west to Redmarshall station. Extension proposed from Redmarshall station north west to the Cleveland/Durham boundary.

CORNWALL

9 **O** Footpath along Wadebridge–Padstow line, with access and picnic places. Public access permitted on whole length of line, except the bridges and embankment across Little Petherick creek.

CUMBRIA

10 **X** Footpath along a 2 mile stretch of Workington–Penrith line, starting at Workington.

11 **X** Public footpath along a mile of the Piel branch, near Roosecote power station. The county council is currently considering a nature walk here. The whole walk is adjacent to the Roosecote sands site of special scientific interest.

DERBYSHIRE

12 **O** Rowsley–Blackwell Mill, near Buxton. This is a former Midland Railway branch along the valley of the River Wye. The 11 mile walkway is proposed by the Peak Park Planning Board.

13 **X** High Peak Trail. (17½ miles) A fully developed trail for walkers, cyclists and horse-riders from Cromford to Buxton, along the former Cromford & High Peak line. It links at the western end with the Tissington trail (see below) at Parsley Hay. Features include station buildings, inclines, steam winding engines and beauty spots. Warden service. Illustrated leaflet available from the Derbyshire County Planning Department. The countryside warden can be contacted at the Engine House, Middleton Top, Wirksworth, Derbyshire. Tel: Wirksworth 3204.

14 **X** The Tissington Trail. (13 miles) Fully developed trail for walkers, horse-riders and cyclists from Ashbourne to Parsley Hay, where it joins the High Peak trail (see above). Facilities at station sites. Ranger service, contacted at Moneystones, Old Station, Hartington, Derbyshire. Illustrated leaflet available from the Information Section, The Peak National Park, Bakewell, Derbyshire.

15 **X** The Sett Valley Trail. Footpath and bridleway (3½ miles) between Hayfield and New Mills.

16 **O** Tibshelf–Holmewood Trail. Bridleway and footpath.

DEVON

17 **O** Footpath along the GWR Plymouth–Tavistock line.

18 **O** Footpath along Yelverton–Princetown branch. Public access already permitted.

19 **O** Footpath along the Cann Quarry Tramway.

20 **O** Footpath along the Barnstaple–Braunton line, as part of the North Devon coast footpath.

21 **O** Footpath along Lyme Regis–Axminster line. Proposed by private group. (See Chapter 9.)

DORSET

22 **O** Bridleway along the Somerset & Dorset Railway line between Blandford Forum and Sturminster Marshall. (See Chapter 8, page 75.)

23 **O** Wimborne–West Moors. Being acquired by Dorset County Council to reserve a route for a possible rapid transit system. When bought and until required for the RTS, the public will be allowed to use the line as a footpath.

24 **X** Part of the Derwent Walk (see Tyne & Wear).

25 **X** Deerness Valley Walk (9 miles) from Durham City to Crook via Esh Winning. One picnic area already, and another planned.

26 **X** Bishop–Brandon Walk (9½ miles) from Durham City to Bishop Auckland via Willington. Impressive viaduct across River Wear ½ mile from Bishop Auckland. Small picnic area at Brancepeth Station. (See Chapter 15.)

27 **X** Waskerley Way (7 miles) from Consett to Stanhope via Waskerley; 3½ miles across open moorland with panoramic views over the Derwent Valley and Weardale. Near Consett is the towering Hounsgill Viaduct. Two small picnic areas and two small car parks. Eventually to be linked at western end to the Lanchester Valley Walk (see below).

28 **O** Lanchester Valley Walk. (12 miles) Along River Browney from Durham City to Consett via Lanchester. Full-time warden living in Lanchester station house, and an information centre here as well. This walkway will link into all the routes detailed above, except the Derwent Walk.

29 **O** Shildon–Bishop Auckland–Barnard Castle. (15½ miles) Barnard Castle is a small, hilly town with some fascinating old buildings and a huge selection of pubs.

30 **O** Bishop Auckland–Spennymoor (5 miles).

31 **O** Barnard Castle–Middleton-in-Teesdale. (7½ miles) Follows the beautiful River Tees.

32 **O** Station Town–Thorpe Thewles. (5½ miles in Co. Durham, 5 miles in Cleveland.)

EAST SUSSEX

33 **X** The Forest Way. Linear country park running 9½ miles from East Grinstead to Groombridge. Resurfaced, and provided with picnic areas, toilets, horse-riding access points, etc. Ranger service. Illustrated leaflet has been produced. Further information from the County Estates Department, Southover House, Southover Road, Lewes, East Sussex BN7 1YA.

34 **O** Bridleway from Heathfield to Hellingly.

35 **X** Footpath from Hellingly to Hailsham (no horses or cycles).

36 **X** The former line between Bexhill and Crowhurst—part of that town's footpath system.

ESSEX
37 **X** Footpath (2½ miles) from Bateman's Tower, Brightlingsea, to Alresford Creek.

GLOUCESTERSHIRE
38 **O** Bridleway along the Cirencester link line from Cirencester to the Wiltshire/Gloucestershire boundary.

GREATER MANCHESTER
39 **O** Middlewood railway footpath and bridleway at Stockport. To be landscaped, planted and provided with facilities.
40 **O** Brinnington railway, Stockport. Landscaped footpath with facilities.
41 **O** Whitworth Road, Rochdale. Short landscaped footpath.
42 **O** Footpath at Gidlow, Standish, Wigan.
On the Stalybridge–Diggle line are several footpath and bridleway schemes.
43 **O** Stalybridge–Scout Quarry.
44 **X** Micklehurst–Roaches, Mossley.
45 **O** Friezeland–Greenfield.
46 **O** Greenfield–Diggle.
47 **O** Delph Spur.

HAMPSHIRE
Hampshire County Council is granting a 'permissive right' to the public on all the sections of disused railway that it acquires. (Other county councils please note.)
48 **O** Bridleway from the Ridgeway route at Litchfield, northwards to Highclere station.
49 **O** Bridleway on the Meon Valley line, from Knowle Junction northwards to Droxford station. From Droxford station northwards to West Meon will be a permissive bridleway until required for road improvement.
50 **O** Test Valley line. Bridleway from Mottisfont station northwards to Fullerton station. Permissive until required for road improvement.

HEREFORD AND WORCESTERSHIRE

51 **X** Brotheridge Green nature reserve (1½ miles). Half-way between former Malvern Wells station and Upton-on-Severn, on Malvern–Tewkesbury line. Very varied plant and bird life, badger setts, foxes, insects and butter-flies (including marbled white, usually associated with the Cotswolds and Mendips, and the South Coast). The reserve is private but walkers will be allowed to enjoy it on application to the Secretary of the Worcestershire Nature Conservation Trust Ltd, Avoncroft, Stoke Heath, Bromsgrove, Worcestershire B6O 4JS.

HERTFORDSHIRE

52 **X** The Cole Greenway. A 4 mile stretch between Hertford and Cole Green station. Footpath and bridle-way, co-ordinated with other footpaths in the area.

53 **O** The Ayot Greenway. A 4 mile footpath and bridleway from Campus West in Welwyn Garden City through Ayot Green to Wheathampstead. Linked to other paths in the Upper Lea Valley.

ISLE OF MAN

54 **O** Footpaths on sections of St John's to Ramsey line (approx. 17 miles).

55 **O** Footpath from St John's to Peel (approx. 3 miles).

ISLE OF WIGHT

56 **O** Newport–Wootton footpath (3 miles).

57 **O** Footpath from Old Cement Mills, Stag Lane to Cowes (2¼ miles). To run alongside and over same route as proposed miniature railway.

58 **X** Thorley Road, Yarmouth to Freshwater footpath (2½ miles).

59 **X** Shanklin to Wroxall footpath (2½ miles).

60 **X** Short footpath (1¼ miles) immediately south of Wroxall station.

61 **X** Great Budbridge Manor bridleway (½ mile).

62 **O** Newchurch to Sandown Waterworks bridleway (2 miles).

LEICESTERSHIRE

63 **X** Battlefield of Bosworth footpath (¾ mile). Runs from Shenton station (restored and used as information point

for the battlefield) to the Ashby de la Zouch Canal, along the top of a cutting which is a nature reserve for part of its length.

LINCOLNSHIRE

64 **X** The Spa Trail, with 4 miles of old railway and 1½ miles of public right of way between Woodhall Spa and Horncastle. Information boards, waymarks, a picnic place and small car parks. The trail is part of the long-distance Viking Way from Humber Bank to Oakham, Leics. (See Chapter 13.)

65 **X** Willoughby to Farlesthorpe Level Crossing. 1½ miles, bought for education and Nature Conservation purposes. Not in use as a public footpath, but access is permitted on application to: The County Secretary, County Offices, Lincoln LN1 1YL. Tel Lincoln (STD 0522) 29931.

The former Lindsey County Council produced a very well illustrated and laid out booklet (Price 90p) entitled *Disused Railways in Lindsey: Policy for after use*—available from the above address.

MERSEYSIDE

66 **X** The Wirral Country Park. See Chapter 10. Details from the Head Ranger, The Wirral Country Park, Station Road, Thurstaston, Wirral, Cheshire L67 0HN. Tel Irby (STD 051-648) 4371.

67 **O** Footpath (1½ miles) from Rookery Lane northwards to Rainford Junction, in St Helens district. Eventually to be extended southward to Moss Bank.

NORFOLK

68 **O** Hellesdon–Drayton footpath and bridleway.

69 **O** King's Lynn–South Wootton footpath and cycleway.

NORTH YORKSHIRE

70 **X** Footpath (16½ miles) from Scarborough to Hawsker Bottoms, along the Scarborough and Whitby railway line.

71 **X** Footpath (1 mile) between the former Richmond station and the bridge over the River Swale at Easby. Incorporated in the Richmond Country Park scheme.

72 **X** Country walk from Parkgate Lane to the former Catterick Bridge station.

73 **X** Footpath along mineral railway up the Ingleby incline from Bank Foot and into the North York Moors National Park.

NOTTINGHAMSHIRE

74 **X** The Southwell Trail. 4½ miles along the Farnsfield to Southwell line. Many facilities (car parks, picnic areas, etc.), and some industrial archaeology remnants. Ranger service. Illustrated leaflet available from the Managing Ranger, The Mill, Rufford Country Park, Ollerton, Newark, Nottinghamshire. Tel Mansfield 823148.

SOMERSET

75 **X** Footpath along 2 mile stretch of the Taunton–Barnstaple line, between Dulverton station and Dennington Lane, Brushford. There are plans to incorporate the path in the Exmoor National Park waymarked walks scheme.

STAFFORDSHIRE

76 **X** Greenways development, Stoke-on-Trent. A complete system of public footpaths, built up on the network of disused lines in the area. Includes the Potteries loop line from Cobridge Park in the south to Goldenhill in the north (part of the well worked out and fascinating Potteries walkway). Also the Westport–Fegg Hayes line walkway, and the Berry Hill–Normacott greenway. The whole city has taken in hand its huge areas of derelict marl pits, spoil heaps and quarries, and renovated them in a massive land reclamation scheme. Illustrated booklets and pamphlets available from the Director of Environmental Services, P.O. Box 207, Unity House, Hanley, Stoke-on-Trent ST1 4QL. Tel Stoke-on-Trent (STD 0782) 29611. (See Chapter 12.)

77 **O** Biddulph Walkway, from Biddulph to Congleton. The northern section near Congleton has already been reclaimed and treated by a group of conservation volunteers, 'Cleanteam', sponsored by the chief planning officer of Staffordshire Moorlands District Council. Other local authorities please note.

78 **X** Manifold Valley route (8½ miles). Footpath along the track of the Leek & Manifold Light Railway between

131

Hulme End and Waterhouses. Interpretive sheet for schools available from the Schools Service, Peak National Park Office, Baslow Road, Bakewell, Derbyshire DE4 1AE. Tel Bakewell 2881.

79 **O** Churnet Valley footpath and bridleway from Leek to the Cheshire boundary. Conversion is currently under way, with car parks and picnic facilities at the former station sites at Rudyard, Cliffe Park and Rushton Spencer. The same conversion programme is planned for the section of line from Oakamore to Denstone, with parking facilities at Denstone, Alton and Oakamoor.

80 **O** Footpath and bridleway along former Stafford–Wellington line, between the M6 Motorway and Haughton Village.

SUFFOLK

81 **X** The Railway Walk, Haverhill (3 miles). A traffic-free, landscaped walk through the centre of the town, running into open countryside at each end. Designed as the spine on which the town's footpath system is built up.

82 **X** Clare Castle Country Park; ½ mile of old railway line has been incorporated in the park.

83 **X** Lavenham Walk (½ mile). Footpath and bridleway.

84 **X** Rodbridge to Sudbury footpath (2½ miles).

85 **X** Hadleigh to Raydon (2½ miles). Footpath with fine views across the Brett Valley.

86 **O** Bull Lane, Long Melford (1½ miles). Used locally as a general recreation area.

SURREY

87 **X** Baynards to Bramley footpath, bridleway and cycling track. (An extension of the Shoreham–Baynards scheme: see WEST SUSSEX).

TYNE AND WEAR

Most disused lines in Tyne and Wear are wagonways (purely mineral lines). Some were worked with stationary engines. Tyne and Wear County Council intends eventually to convert them all.

88 **X** The Derwent Walk Country Park. 10½ miles from Swalwell to Blackhill, Consett, along the Derwent Valley line. Four viaducts, and much else of interest. Ranger service. Illustrated pamphlet available from Tyne and

Wear County Council Planning Department, Sandyford House, Newcastle-upon-Tyne NE2 1ED.

89 **X** Bridleway (1 mile) at Monkseaton station, Whitley Bay. To be extended northwards.

90 **O** Bridleway through linear park at Rising Sun colliery, Battlehill, Wallsend, on track of Rising Sun wagonway. Largely suburban in character.

91 **O** Bridleways and footpaths from Hetton-le-Hole to Pilkington station, on former Eppleton–Durham wagonway.

92 **O** Bridleways and footpaths from Low Moorsley to Houghton-le-Spring, on former Moorsley wagonway.

93 **O** Footpath and bridleway from Silksworth colliery to Ryhope village on the track of the wagonway.

94 **O** Countryside route on the Bowes Railway from Kibblesworth colliery west to Marley Hill. The Kibblesworth to Springwell portions are being restored as working inclines.

95 **O** Bridleway along river from Newburn to Wylam, on track of former North Wylam Railway. This route is administered jointly with Northumberland County Council.

96 **O** Countryside route from Barmston to Sunderland airport and Hylton bridge. This is the first part of a scheme for a complete route past Boldon.

97 **O** Town and country route from Gateshead to Sunniside, along the Tanfield wagonway. Above Sunniside the line is to be used by a steam preservation society.

98 **O** Urban bridleway at Felling, along the Pelaw wagonway.

WARWICKSHIRE

99 **O** Bridleway along the Kenilworth to Berkswell line, possibly providing a link to a country park or picnic site alongside the line.

WEST MIDLANDS

100 **O** Leisure walkway along the Harborne branch line, Birmingham. A short section at the northern end has already been reclaimed. (Walkway will be 2 miles long overall.) For further information contact the Birmingham City Planning Department, P.O. Box 28, 120 Edmund Street, Birmingham B3 2RD.

101 **X** Shoreham to Baynards via Christ's Hospital (18 miles). A bridleway, cleared, resurfaced, drained and sign-posted, has been created from Steyning, 2 miles north of Shoreham, to Baynards. A 1½ mile stretch at Slinfold, south of Baynards, has been converted to a nature trail and reserve. The Sussex Naturalist Trust has written a Nature Trail Guide, primarily for children, obtainable from the County Valuer, County Hall, Chichester, West Sussex PO19 1RQ. (See Chapter 10.)

102 **O** The Worth Way. 5½ miles of bridleway from Three Bridges to East Grinstead, linking up with the Forest Way. (See EAST SUSSEX.)

WEST YORKSHIRE

103 **O** Footpath and bridleway along the Chevet branch (2¼ miles).

WILTSHIRE

104 **X** Calne, alongside River Marden. Short stretch of foot-path diverted on to railway line and used as nature trail.

105 **O** Footpath from Marlborough High Level station to Granham farm.

106 **O** Cricklade (Horsey Down) to the Gloucestershire county boundary. Footpath and bridleway access to the Cotswold water park. This scheme is administered jointly with Gloucestershire County Council.

107 **O** Chiseldon to Ogbourne St George. Acquired by Wilt-shire County Council for long-term highway improve-ments to the A345. Public access on foot and horseback is permitted.

England—London Boroughs

BARNET
108 **O** Walkway along the Mill Hill East to Edgware branch line.

ENFIELD
109 **X** Plevna Road walkway (¾ mile). Laid out with trees in 1973 by parks department. Badly vandalised, and replanted in 1975.

HAMMERSMITH
110 **X** Leisure gardens and children's play area on disused line at Emlyn Gardens, W12.

HARINGEY
111 **O** Parkland Walk. (See ISLINGTON.)
112 **O** Palace Gates railway walk.

HARROW
113 **X** Wealdstone to Stanmore branch line owned by the borough, and used by residents as a footpath linking Harrow's leisure centre, the shops in Wealdstone High Street, Belmont Circle and Stanmore. Regrading of path and access improvements are planned.

ISLINGTON
114 **O** Parkland Walk. A 2 mile 'biological corridor' along the railway between Crouch End and Muswell Hill in the Borough of Haringey. To be resurfaced, landscaped and planted.

SOUTHWARK
115 **O** Walkway on short section of the Nunhead to Crystal Palace High Level line, north east of Dulwich Wood.

Scotland

CENTRAL
116 **O** Footpath link between Dollar and Tillicoultry. Part of the Hillfoots Walk.
117 **O** Linear Park on a filled-in cutting between New Sauchie and Fishcross, on the northern outskirts of Alloa.

DUMFRIES AND GALLOWAY

118 **O** Long-distance footpath (10 miles) on the Dumfries to
Stranraer line, between Mossdale and Gatehouse station.
The route crosses the Laughenghie site of special scientific interest, and the Cairnsmore of Fleet national nature
reserve.

FIFE

119 **X** The Boblingen Way in Glenrothes New Town, along
the track of the Markinch to Leslie line. A cycle track is
to be incorporated with the footpath.

GRAMPIAN

120 **X** Deeside line footpaths and bridleways between
Aberdeen and Culter, and between Cambus O'May and
Ballater (see Chapter 6). Each stretch is 4 miles long.
The station and booking office at Cambus O'May are to
be converted to an interpretive centre based on the
history of this very beautiful stretch of line, formerly
patronised by the royal family on journeys to Balmoral.
Ballater station will also be restored.

HIGHLAND

121 **O** Boat of Garten to Elgin long-distance footpath. (Boat
of Garten station itself is part of privately-run Strathspey
Railway.)

LOTHIAN

122 **X** Slateford to Juniper Green nature trail (2¾ miles),
along Balerno branch. Part of the long-distance Waters
of Leith Walkway, which will eventually run from the
Pentlands to the Forth. Waymarked points of interest,
nature study, industrial archaeology on this riverside
walk. Ranger service. Illustrated pamphlet and guide
available from the Planning Department of Edinburgh
District Council.

123 **X** Pencaitland Railway Walk, from the County Boundary
at Elphinstone to Saltoun station (5 miles). Ranger
service. Facilities. Hand-written and drawn pamphlet
available from Lothian County Planning Department.
(See Chapter 16.)

124 **O** Lesmahagow walkway along part of old line between Stonehouse and Altdon Heights, Lesmahagow.

125 **X** Cumnock walkway, providing a pedestrian link between two residential areas. Includes a red sandstone viaduct across the Glaisnock Water.

126 **O** Walkway (1½ miles) at the Monkland Canal, Brownsburn, to the centre of Airdrie, creating a footpath link with the village of Calderbank.

127 **X** Walkway at Kilmarnock, starting at Crosshouse and finishing in Cunninghame District.

128 **X** Country walk beside the River Irvine from Hurlford, near Kilmarnock, to Priestland.

129 **O** Footpath linking East Kilbride town centre to the industrial estate.

130 **O** Jamestown to Croftamie walkway.

131 **O** East End, Dumbarton, walkway.

132 **X** Chapelhall footpath, Motherwell—rehabilitated and landscaped.

133 **X** Victoria Park walkway, Glasgow (800yd). Play area; planted and landscaped. A continuation to Crow Road is planned, and eventually the whole walkway will be linked to the Parkland trunk route system.

134 **X** Kilsyth walkway (¾ mile). Runs from Kilsyth central park—the Burngreen—eastwards to the Colzium Lennox estate (a Georgian house and grounds open to the public).

135 **X** Milton of Campsie parkland area. A joint venture by Strathkelvin and Stirling District Councils. Part of a proposed footpath from Milton of Campsie to Kirkintilloch.

136 **O** Torrance to Bardowie walkway, giving access to the countryside. Eventually to be extended to the northern outskirts of Glasgow.

137 **O** Lennoxtown to Strathblane walkway.

138 **O** Stirling to Croftamie walkway.

TAYSIDE

139 **O** Countryside walk at Arbroath, from Colliston (Letham Grange) station to St Vigeans.

140 **O** Footpath between Borrowfield housing estate and Montrose town centre.

Wales

141 **X** Lower Wye Valley walk. Part of this outstandingly beautiful 16 mile waymarked route between Chepstow and Monmouth is on the disued Wye Valley branch from Tintern station northwards. Tintern station has been developed as an information and railway exhibition centre, with a picnic area, car parks, refreshments, and a schedule of walks starting from the station and led by the countryside wardens. Illustrated pamphlets available from Tintern Station, Tintern, Gwent.

142 **O** Public right of way from Mayhill (Monmouth) to Hadnock. 1½ miles, along the former Monmouth to Ross branch line.

143 **O** Waymarked footpath at Wyllie, in the Sirhowy valley, on the former Newport to Tredegar line.

GWYNEDD

144 **O** Long-distance footpath from Dinas, Llandwa to Porthmadog, along the trackbed of the Welsh Highland Railway; 11½ miles are in use as a footpath already, and the rest is to be acquired and restored.

145 **X** Mawddach estuary footpath from Penmaenpool to Morfa Mawddach.

MID GLAMORGAN

146 **X** Footpath between Dynea and Nantgarw in the Taff valley. Part of proposed Taff valley trunk footpath. Cleared by the voluntary efforts of local schoolchildren.

POWYS

147 **O** Govilon railway walk (3 miles), from Llanfoist to Gilwern. Scheme to be carried out by the Brecon Beacons National Park Committee.

SOUTH GLAMORGAN

148 **O** Footpath and cycleway in central Cardiff, linking the housing areas of Splott and Tremorfa with the public open space of Roath Park and lake.

WEST GLAMORGAN

149 **O** Footpath from Port Talbot to Bryn village (3 miles).

150 **O** Footpath along the old Glasbrook Mineral Railway, extending 1½ miles eastwards from Gowerton village. Local inhabitants already claim the line as a right of way.

151 **O** The former Rhondda & Swansea Bay Railway, running through Afan Argoed country park. Two plans are being discussed:

(a) to turn the line and associated land into a linear extension of the park;

(b) to use the line exclusively as a bridleway.

APPENDIX B
Some useful addresses

THE BRANCH LINE SOCIETY
c/o The Secretary,
15 Springwood Hall Gardens,
Gledholt,
Huddersfield,
Yorkshire HD1 4HA.

BRITISH RAILWAYS BOARD
222 Marylebone Road,
London NW1 6JJ

COUNCIL FOR NATURE
c/o Zoological Gardens,
Regent's Park,
London NW1.
(The Council for Nature will supply addresses of local Natural History Societies and County Naturalists' Trusts.)

THE COUNTRYSIDE COMMISSION
John Dower House,
Cresent Place,
Cheltenham,
Glos. GL50 3RA.

THE COUNTRYSIDE COMMISSION FOR SCOTLAND
Battleby,
Redgorton,
Perth PH1 3EW
Scotland.

THE RAILWAY RAMBLERS
c/o Nigel Willis,
11 Milverton Avenue,
Leicester LE4 0HY.

THE RAMBLERS' ASSOCIATION
1/4 Crawford Mews,
York Street,
London W1H 1PT.

THE RAILWAY MAGAZINE
Dorset House,
Stamford Street,
London SE1 9LU.

ACKNOWLEDGEMENTS

I am indebted to many people and sources in gathering material for this book. In particular I would like to thank British Rail for permission to use the information from the maps on pages 66–67 and 144–145 of *Rail 150*, edited by Jack Simmons and published by Methuen Paperbacks; the editor of *Railway Magazine*, J. N. Slater, for permission to use material previously published in that magazine, for patiently answering my many questions, and for publishing in June 1976 my article 'Silk Purses from Sows' Ears' which gave rise to this book; David & Charles for permission to quote from *Victorian Stations* by Gordon Biddle; the County Borough of Derby Museum and Art Gallery for permission to quote findings from a list of flora recorded by C. B. Waite, and published as 'Habitat Study No 20' in *Flora of Derbyshire;* the Botany Department, Aberdeen University for permission to quote findings from their 1973 report on the flora and fauna of the Deeside line; Bath City Architect and Planning Officer for permission to quote from the Preliminary Report on the Lyncombe Vale Nature Trail; and David Shepherd for permission to quote from the Guide to the East Somerset Railway.

For permission to print their photographs: Ivo Peters; the Head Ranger and Graham Hutt of the Wirral Country Park; Department of Environmental Services, Stoke-on-Trent; T. A. S. Parkins; The Exmoor Press; County Planning Department, West Midlands County Council; Captain E. A. Gibbs, R.N; the County Planning Department, Durham County Council; and Christopher Dunne.

My thanks are also due to all the County Councils of England, Wales and Scotland, and to all the London Borough Councils, for so generously supplying me with the facts, figures, pamphlets, maps and drawings that enabled me to compile Appendix A; to Frank White, who braved a freezing December day to show me round the Wirral Country Park; to my wife, who keeps me going; and to Lord Beeching, without whom this book would never have been written.

C.S.

BIBLIOGRAPHY AND FURTHER READING

Railways

Appleton, Dr J. II. *Disused Railways in the Countryside of England and Wales* (Report to the Countryside Commission), HMSO (1970)

Atthill, Robin *The Picture History of the Somerset & Dorset Railway*, David & Charles (1970)

Atthill, Robin *The Somerset & Dorset Railway*, David & Charles (1967)

Biddle, Gordon *Victorian Stations*, David & Charles (1973)

Clinker, C. R. *Clinker's Register of Closed Stations*

Coleman, Terry *The Railway Navvies*, Penguin Books (Pelican) (1970)

Forgotten Railways series (*Chilterns and Cotswolds, East Midlands, North-East England, North and Mid-Wales, Scotland, East Anglia, South-East England* already published, others planned), David & Charles

Haresnape, Brian *Railway Design Since 1830*, 2 Vols, Ian Allan (1968/9)

Parham, E. T. *Disused Railway Lines in Scotland—A Strategic Appraisal* (Report to the Countryside Commission for Scotland), HMSO (1972)

Peters, Ivo *The Somerset & Dorset—An English Cross Country Railway*, Oxford Publishing Co (1974)

Railway History Map of Britain, John Bartholomew & Son Ltd (1974)

The Railway Magazine, various articles

Regional History of the Railways of Great Britain series, David & Charles

Simmons, Jack, ed, *Rail 150—The Stockton & Darlington Railway and what followed*, Eyre Methuen (1975)

143

Symes, Rodney & Cole, David *Railway Architecture of Greater London*, Osprey Publishing Ltd (1973)
Symes, Rodney & Cole, David *Railway Architecture of the south-east*, Osprey Publishing Ltd (1972)

For Children

Anderson, John F. *The Railway Book*, London Museum Press Ltd (1963)
Bowood, Richard *The Story of Railways*, Ladybird (Achievements Series 601) (1961)

General

Campaign for Real Ale *The Good Beer Guide*, Arrow Books (1975)
Chinery, Michael *A Field Guide to the Insects of Britain and Northern Europe*, Collins (1973)
Fitter, Richard, Fitter, Alastair & Blamey, Marjorie *The Wild Flowers of Britain and Northern Europe*, Collins (1974)
Hillaby, John *Journey through Britain*, Paladin (1970)
Mitchell, Alan *A Field Guide to the Trees of Britain and Northern Europe*, Collins (1974)
Peterson, Mountfort, & Hollom, *A Field Guide to the Birds of Britain and Europe*, Collins (3rd ed. 1974)

144